BOUNDARIES

By the same author

Shifting the Paradigms of The Normal Christian Church (1994)

Baptism in Water & The Spirit (Oikos Books, 1995, 2008)

Lord of All (Oikos Books, 2002)

A New Kind of Baptist Church–Reframing Congregational Government for the 21st Century (Morling Press, 2010)

The Want Me to Be an Elder–What do They Do? (Oikos Books, 2018)

BOUNDARIES

Rediscovering the Ten Commandments
for the Twenty-First Century

BRIAN N. WINSLADE

Foreword by Leith Anderson

RESOURCE *Publications* · Eugene, Oregon

BOUNDARIES
Rediscovering the Ten Commandments for the Twenty-First Century

Resource Publications
An Imprint of Wipf and Stock Publishers
199 W. 8th Ave., Suite 3
Eugene, OR 97401

www.wipfandstock.com

PAPERBACK ISBN: 978-1-5326-6530-1
HARDCOVER ISBN: 978-1-5326-6531-8
EBOOK ISBN: 978-1-5326-6532-5

Manufactured in the U.S.A.   11/06/18

To my grandchildren . . .
Growing up in a world of moral relativity,
unanchored from objective truth

Contents

Foreword

MOST READERS SKIP THE Foreword to a book. That is okay if you want to get right into taking a fresh look at the Ten Commandments for the 21st Century. For those who choose to read a page before Brian Winslade's chapters begin, here is the first word: *The Ten Commandments are extraordinary and unparalleled in human experience.*

The ten commandments answer the most basic universal question "How are we supposed to live?" More than three millennia ago the people of Israel were miraculously liberated from generations of harsh slavery. That was the good news. The difficult news was that they didn't know how to live. They may have known how to build pyramids, suffer beatings and watch their sons being slaughtered but they had no idea how to thrive and proposer as the free people of God. They had a lot to learn and needed a simple yet comprehensive place to begin. So, God called their leader to the top of Mount Sinai and gave them a list of ten principles to guide all of their lives.

The ten commandments work everywhere for everyone. Visit a foreign culture or read a history book to quickly discover the complexity and variety of human experiences and ethics. In a world with billions of individuals who speak different languages and come from contradictory traditions, it seems impossible to prepare a short list of ethical standards that fit everyone, everywhere in every generation.

Coming up with any standards that apply to those who are ancient and modern, poor and prosperous, female and male, younger and older, uneducated and educated, primitive and modern, violent and peaceful, victorious and defeated, sad and happy, and thousands more variations . . . well, the assignment goes to the top of a page of impossible tasks.

The Ten Commandments accomplished the impossible. They are short, profound, universal and transformative. They can be read, understood and memorized by the simplest child and by the most sophisticated adult. It is no wonder that these ten have been translated into almost every known language and revered for thousands of years as the standard of good and godly living. There is nothing else like them.

The ten commandments are especially for Christians. While they have permeated most religions and are an ethical and behavioral gold standard for everyone everywhere, the Ten Commandments are paramount for Christians.

Like the first recipients who heard God's ten precepts, Christians are those who have been set free. Israel was saved from Egypt by a miracle that changed everything; Christians have been saved from sin by the miracle of Jesus that has changed everything. We both faced the same challenge of how to live faithfully and gratefully in the name of the Lord who saved us. God gave us all the Ten Commandments.

Now we turn the page to live these amazing supernatural Ten Commandments here in our twenty-first century.

Leith Anderson
President
National Association of Evangelicals
Washington, DC USA

Preface

WE LIVE IN AN interesting age and there are many characteristics that distinguish the beginning of this twenty-first century of human history from the centuries that preceded it. For example, the emergence of a global economy, the development of digital technologies, and our ability to access information through the internet. Another defining characteristic of this age might be our accelerated progress toward moral relativity. Morality and ethics once had an immutable foundation—they were something to be measured against, in which we could place our trust, and which therefore influenced our choices and behavior. Truth was objective and absolute, not something to be challenged or questioned.

Those days are long gone, particularly in the developed world. We had "facts" about events in time and space, and alongside these we now have "alternative facts" describing the same thing but with different metrics. This has implications for a post-post-modern worldview, wherein fields as diverse as philosophy, medicine, law, science, and economics, we appear to have thrown off the shackles of a fixed morality. Nothing is spared the opportunity, indeed the invitation, to critique or adjust our ethical compass. Morality and values are relative to circumstances and popular opinion, and the majority voice is the primary indicator for establishing right from wrong.

But it hasn't always been this way. In fact, one does not need to go back too far in human history to a time when moral values were defined, clearly enunciated and the bedrock of a civil society.

Just where our contemporary era of moral relativity will lead is anyone's guess. Is it progressing towards a more enlightened and tolerant civilization as some might claim, or is it leading our culture into insecurity and chaos? Might it even be that within the current moral vacuum there is an emergent desire for the restoration of the ageless values upon which previous generations based their behavior and society?

The book you're holding is about the Ten Commandments which God gave to the nation of Israel as it formed in the desert, having recently escaped from Egypt and now *en route* to their promised land. Over the centuries these commandments have formed the basis of moral, relationship, and property law for countless civilizations. They were widely accepted and virtually unchallenged and can be considered a bit like "boundary rules" for the "game of life." Play within the boundaries, and there is freedom, but step outside of the boundaries and the consequences can be dire.

In an age of moral relativity, the question is often raised: how relevant are they for today's world? Indeed, even among those who identify themselves as followers of Jesus Christ, are they still regarded as immutable boundaries to live within, or have they been superseded? These are the kinds of questions this book seeks to explore.

Many of the commandments given to Moses all those years ago were refined by Jesus in his famous Sermon on the Mount. Apparently, it is not only in our contemporary age that their substance and essence has been tampered with. In many instances Jesus needed to highlight God's original intention and bring clarity to our understanding of the Ten Commandments, making them all the more poignant for those who follow him today.

Who is this book for? Three distinct audiences are envisaged.

Firstly, it is aimed at Christians who are keen to wrestle with an ancient, yet timeless, section of God's word. Understood fully, the Ten Commandments are an essential discipleship resource which we should be familiar with; allowing it to change the way we think and behave. While their origins were in a specific time and place, their application is pertinent across all cultures and circumstances. If you are a follower of Jesus Christ, the pages of this book are written with you in mind.

Secondly, it is offered as a resource for dialogue and discussion. Perhaps a small group could read a chapter a week and discuss together the applications in their everyday lives? Undoubtedly not everything contained in this book will be agreeable to every reader. The objective, however, is to provide a prompt for reflection and to begin a conversation about our motivations and commitment to live life "the Jesus way" in light of the boundaries God gave in his Ten Commandments.

Thirdly, it is a resource for pastors, and hopefully a prompt for preaching through the Ten Commandments in the churches they serve. Might it be that some of the ancient literature from the earliest years of the Israelite community have been deemed a tad difficult, perhaps even controversial, for some? Maybe these expositions of each value statement God gave to his chosen people could act as a starting point or resource that you could add to and share more widely.

May God grant us all his grace and mercy as we handle the written record of his dealings with the human race and live within the wise boundaries he has set for us.

Brian N. Winslade
2018

Acknowledgments

THE IMPETUS FOR THIS book is not my own. It all began as a sermon series in the church I serve as pastor. Within our congregation over recent years, has sat an eminent theologian who has become a dear friend and mentor, Dr. Murray J. Harris, who was insistent that I explore its publication. Dr. Harris has a distinguished career as a theologian and academic of note around the world (including teaching for many years at Trinity Evangelical Divinity School, Warden of Tyndale House in Cambridge, author of numerous commentaries, and a leading translator of the New International Version of the Bible). I gladly and gratefully acknowledge his advice and encouragement to embark upon this project.

Next, I needed to find someone with editorial skills. I felt prompted to approach Jenny Holland, a member of my church and a school teacher, only to discover that she also works as a skilled editor of technical textbooks, and has a theological degree in her own right. Not only was she able to guide my transition from spoken-word to written-prose, we also had some invaluable theological discussions on a number of ideas I was proposing.

An author is seldom able to copy-edit their own work, so my deepest gratitude also goes to Chris Gardner (former newspaper editor), Tiffany Sayer, and Kitty Lester, all of whom are great friends with a skilled eye for detail.

Finally, I acknowledge the help and guidance of Matthew Wimer and the editors at Resource Publications of Wipf and Stock for helping this book come into being. May its pages bring glory to God and deeper maturity amongst those who, like me, follow Jesus Christ.

Chapter 1

Behavior Boundaries

TALKBACK RADIO IS A major component of audio broadcasting in the twenty-first century and is at times deliberately contentious. On occasion, it can fascinate and enlighten the opinions of supposedly average citizens in a society. At other times, it leads to embarrassment and shame at sharing citizenship with some of the opinionated nonsense that gets phoned in! A disproportionate amount of discussion on talkback radio focuses on the role governments play in regulating (or deregulating) what people can and cannot do. Some advocate for a *nanny-state* with rules and laws for everything; others project a more *civil-libertarian* agenda, arguing in favor of minimal legislation and more personal choice.

Regardless of one's stance on social debates of this nature, over the past 100 years there has certainly been a lot of rethinking about the moral codes and ethical values that govern developed societies. Many values, once taught as self-evident and immutable, are being rethought or are no longer regarded as absolute or even relevant. Questions are raised as to whether there is room anymore for absolute moral codes by which everyone should live, and by which it is possible to determine right from wrong.

The goal posts of moral law have certainly shifted considerably over the past few decades and morality is becoming increasingly based upon current popular consensus, rather than an objective time-honored standard. For instance, if enough people think the age for purchasing alcohol should be lowered, or marijuana decriminalized, or speed limits increased, then the law is changed. Determining right behavior from wrong behavior in a post-modern twenty-first-century world rests upon this type of consensus and doesn't appear to be anchored to anything solid.

By way of an analogy, if individual lives were likened to a series of boats floating on "the sea of life," it could be argued that their moral anchors have been pulled up from anything solid on the seabed and their boats are merely tied to each other—giving the illusion of safety. Together they drift on the tide of popular opinion. Whatever the majority believe is right, becomes permissible behavior, and is potentially passed into law.

What are followers of Jesus Christ to make of all this?

In short, the Bible (as the primary source for understanding God's will) offers a rather different perspective. The worldview of the Bible suggests that God has offered the people of planet Earth an objective standard by which to live and determine what is, and what is not, acceptable behavior. Three and a half thousand years ago, by means of divine revelation, God gave humanity ten principles or core values by which they should live. We know them today as the Ten Commandments or the *Decalogue*. They are recorded in the Old Testament in two places: Exodus 20 and Deuteronomy 5. The objective of this book is to examine each of these value statements and to explore their relevance and their implications for the contemporary world in which we live.

The Ten Commandments are a series of statements given by God that offer an objective basis (we could call them anchors) for determining right from wrong. They are like a set of core values for humanity. Exodus 20 records them this way:

> And God spoke all these words:
>
> 2 "I am the LORD your God, who brought you out of Egypt, out of the land of slavery.
>
> 3 "You shall have no other gods before me.

4 "You shall not make for yourself an image in the form of anything in heaven above or on the earth beneath or in the waters below. 5 You shall not bow down to them or worship them; for I, the LORD your God, am a jealous God, punishing the children for the sin of the parents to the third and fourth generation of those who hate me, 6 but showing love to a thousand generations of those who love me and keep my commandments.

7 "You shall not misuse the name of the LORD your God, for the LORD will not hold anyone guiltless who misuses his name.

8 "Remember the Sabbath day by keeping it holy. 9 Six days you shall labor and do all your work, 10 but the seventh day is a sabbath to the LORD your God. On it you shall not do any work, neither you, nor your son or daughter, nor your male or female servant, nor your animals, nor any foreigner residing in your towns. 11 For in six days the LORD made the heavens and the earth, the sea, and all that is in them, but he rested on the seventh day. Therefore the LORD blessed the Sabbath day and made it holy.

12 "Honor your father and your mother, so that you may live long in the land the LORD your God is giving you.

13 "You shall not murder.

14 "You shall not commit adultery.

15 "You shall not steal.

16 "You shall not give false testimony against your neighbor.

17 "You shall not covet your neighbor's house. You shall not covet your neighbor's wife, or his male or female servant, his ox or donkey, or anything that belongs to your neighbor."

Exodus 20:1–17

As with any passage of Scripture, acquiring a true understanding requires investigation of the original setting or context in which it is found. While it might be said that the Ten Commandments have become the basis of law in many societies around the world, they were originally given to a specific group of people at a particular place and time in history.

In short, they were a set of moral codes given to a disparate group of recently-liberated slaves, most of whom were probably uneducated and illiterate, and who were living at the time in the desert. Many years before, God had selected a man called Abraham whose offspring were to be a special nation in the eyes of the Lord. The Hebrew people were to become especially close to the Lord, and a community through whom the will of God would be worked out in the world.[1] For several hundred years they lived a hard life in Egypt. They were treated as slaves and greatly oppressed. Through a series of dramatic miracles, and under the leadership of Moses, God rescued them and brought them out of Egypt. He was giving them a new promised land where they would be a nation in their own right. These moral codes or principles of life were like a charter or a constitution for the new nation. A new community of God's people was forming. God, at the point of initiating a covenantal relationship with them, was providing them with boundaries for their attitudes, conduct, and interpersonal relationships, that would allow them to prosper. It was as if God was saying to them, "Live within these boundaries or guidelines and life will go well for you. Step outside of them, or disregard these values, and the fabric of your community will begin to unravel."[2]

The big question to consider concerning a passage of Scripture like the Ten Commandments is how relevant they are for the twenty-first century? While these values were pertinent for a group of people 3500 years ago, are they still applicable in our context today, or are they just a quaint piece of ancient history?

Some obviously think the Ten Commandments are way past their use-by date. Contemporary scholars and ethicists have

1. Genesis 12:1–4
2. Deuteronomy 11

objected to the continued use of ancient values in a contemporary world. The cultures way back then, and now, are vastly different they say, and the values of an ancient past don't fit with contemporary wisdom or a supposedly more enlightened view of life.

There are some who read the Ten Commandments as being unhelpfully negative. They are predominantly a list of *"Don't"* or *"Thou shalt not."* What we need today, they say, are positive statements of *"How to"* or *"You can"* rather than restrictive commands.

Then there are those who object to the idea of an outside source imposing their values onto other people. What authority does God or religion have to determine what is right and what is wrong for all? Surely today we have the freedom and liberty to choose our own moral values for ourselves.

On the other side of the argument, there are those who believe the Ten Commandments provide immutable, absolute values for every culture and society. They might have originally been given in ancient times to a group of relatively uneducated ex-slaves in an arid desert, but their relevance is applicable across all cultures. They cite Jesus' statement in the Sermon on the Mount as proof that the Ten Commandments are still relevant for Christians of all generations.

> 17 Do not think that I have come to abolish the Law or the Prophets; I have not come to abolish them but to fulfill them. 18 For truly I tell you, until heaven and earth disappear, not the smallest letter, not the least stroke of a pen, will by any means disappear from the Law until everything is accomplished.
>
> Matthew 5:17,18

In other words, if Jesus regarded the Old Testament law as relevant, its pertinence for today is confirmed.

Perhaps another compelling reason for believing the Ten Commandments still apply is the shared experience of those to whom they were originally given, and the situation of Christians in every generation. God gave a set of values and laws to the people whom he has rescued from the oppression of slavery.

> 2 I am the LORD your God, who brought you out of Egypt, out of the land of slavery.

> Exodus 20:2

They were laws or a moral code for a people living under a new regime or government. They had effectively changed citizenship. No longer were they living in Egypt; they had to learn a new way of living.

Arguably, something similar has happened to those who follow Jesus Christ today. Christian conversion might be likened to having been liberated from a kind of slavery or bondage to sin, and freedom from its clutches.[3] Jesus' death on the cross perpetually breaks the power of sin, and when his people submit to his lordship he affects liberation from old masters. However, as newly liberated people, Christ-followers must adopt a new set of values. There is a new code to live by. Citizenship changes even though one still lives within this world. The ethical standards or moral codes of God's kingdom are what is described in the Ten Commandments. Sometimes the values and standards of God's kingdom are very different from, or stricter than, those of the world in which we live.

Then there are some people who argue that the historical commandments attributed to God paint him in a bad light. They argue that God's values are portrayed as restrictive or limiting, inhibiting freedom or fun. God therefore, comes to be viewed as a mean, bitter, old judge because he lists certain behaviors as forbidden and commands us not to indulge in them.

In contradistinction to such a view, could it not be argued that the laws of the Lord have the opposite effect? The Ten Commandments are not given to curb or limit freedom but to create it. The moral code of God is not about inhibiting but about enhancing freedom. Some have even called the commandments expressions of love. God loves us so much that he has given us wise boundaries that protect our freedom and make the world safe to live in.

3. Galatians 5:1

To argue that God's laws restrict fun, or that they inhibit freedom, is like saying the bridges would be better off without barriers on the outside lanes. Take the harbor bridges in international cities like San Francisco, Sydney, New York, or Auckland and imagine the barriers removed. "After all, they block our view. They're an insult to our intelligence and are unnecessary. We don't need safety barriers like this. We have freedom and liberty to choose how and where to drive!" How many would drive in the outside lanes of the bridge if the boundary barriers weren't there?

Speaking at a national youth conference in New Zealand in 1983, Tony Campolo told the story of a group of liberal educators who once tried an experiment with kindergarten children and their playground. They took away all the boundary fences around the property because they were perceived to create harmful restrictions on children as they played and learned personal responsibility. By removing them they hoped that children would feel the freedom of having no barriers and develop their own values and limits on their play. An interesting thing happened. The children tended to huddle in the center of the playground and showed signs of deep insecurity in their play. Then they put the boundary fences back, and again something really interesting happened. The children began to play all over the playground, even right up to the edges of the property that were now bounded by fences. In his book, "The Power Delusion," Campolo cites sociological research that is without clearly defined norms and rules to govern life, people become self-destructive and even suicidal.[4]

Boundary fences don't inhibit freedom; they create it. Likewise, with moral codes. God didn't give the newly forming nation of Israel the Ten Commandments to destroy their fun or restrict their freedom. The reverse is actually true. God gave his people boundaries and laws to live within as an expression of love, because he wants life to be enjoyed. Granted, sometimes boundary fences hurt when we run into them or collide with them, but their purpose is to protect us and liberate us to live life to its fullest potential.

4. Campolo, Anthony, Jr, *The Power Delusion*, p.35

So, in each chapter of this book, a closer look is taken at each of these ten moral codes to see where their contemporary impact might lie. To begin with, we consider the first commandment:

3 You shall have no other gods before me.

Exodus 20:3

God's charter or constitution for his chosen people begins with himself. To live within the boundaries of God's kingdom requires the adoption of an exclusive allegiance to God. To him alone. No compromise is allowed. There is to be no mixing of religious belief. When God is our God there is room for no other.

Three and a half thousand years later it's easy to miss the impact of this commandment on the minds of those who first heard it. In the culture of the day, this was a very radical departure from the accepted norm. A technical term to describe the religious worldview of many ancient cultures might be *polytheism* (*poly* meaning "many" and *the-* as a root meaning "god"). In the minds of the surrounding nations, there were many gods at hand who needed to be worshipped, appeased or placated.

Polytheistic religion was understood and expressed in two main ways. The first was that virtually everything on Earth was governed or controlled by a god of some description. There was the "god of the forest" or the "god of the sea" or the "god of night or day." There were gods for fertility and harvest. There were gods for war or trading or hunting, and so forth. Each of these gods exercised power over aspects of a person's life. If you pleased the gods they blessed you. If you displeased the gods they punished you. Therefore, to keep on the good side of all these gods there were myriads of rituals and sacrifices that needed to be performed. The underpinning philosophy of theism (or god-consciousness) was predicated on fear. The gods were not necessarily perceived as friendly or approachable; more often they were easily offended and in need of appeasement.

A second way that polytheism expressed itself in ancient cultures was in a form of religious nationalism, as depicted by the theological term *henotheism*.[5] This refers to belief or allegiance to one god, without denying the existence of other gods. A nation or culture could have its own specific god or gods, while other nations or cultures had different religious deities. In ancient cultures there were many gods, but each people group or nation had their own, which they worshipped and to which they submitted.

So, when God gave the fledgling Israelite nation a moral code to live by, he declared that all notions of *polytheism* were off limits or illegal. Belonging to God's community meant a renunciation of *polytheism* and the adoption of *monotheism*: "There are to be no other Gods but me." God would not share allegiance or attention or focus with any other. The relationship they were to have with God was to be totally exclusive. Yahweh would not climb up on the shelf and sit alongside all the other deities. The God of Israel didn't take his turn amidst other gods. He alone was to be the focus of the people who followed him.

Surrounded by the religious philosophy of *henotheism*, the first commandment meant much more than Yahweh is the God of the Israelites, while all other nations had their different gods. Monotheism declares, "there is only one God for all peoples of the world—period!" There is a form of *henotheism* that still exists in the world today. It's the notion that our world is made up of a mosaic of religious persuasions that are all basically equal in value. For instance, in the Middle East or Northern Africa, they have the Muslim god of Allah. In South East Asian countries there is the god Buddha. In India there are all the Hindu deities. In Western or European cultures there is the God Jesus. A school of thought exists, even amongst some Christians, that theological pluralism and the practice of religious tolerance is the order of the day. Therefore, we merely accept the fact that different cultures have a different religious persuasion. To try and challenge or persuade people of different faiths to adopt or convert to our religious belief system does violence to established religious experience.

To be crystal clear, an understanding of the first commandment offers a rather different view. When God says, there are to

5. Urdang and Flexner, "Henotheism," p.617

be no other gods but me, he is not merely talking about cultures historically influenced by Judeo-Christian theology. He is talking globally. The Christian view of *monotheism* implies a call to mission. It implies a challenge to communicate with and convince all the other peoples of this world that there is only one God. Every other so-called god or deity in our world is a false, or even a demonic spirit. Any allegiance offered to such a god is improper and out of place.

God demands unmitigated allegiance. He will not share his altar with anyone or anything else. The idea is related to the concept of the exclusive loyalty expected within a marriage. This metaphor of God's relationship with his chosen people is repeated throughout both the Old and New Testaments. In their marriage vows a husband and wife promise to forsake or ignore any other person in favor of being exclusively faithful to their spouse. When God laid out his moral code for his people, the first clause was that he, and he alone, would be their God.

In the minds of some people, this kind of exclusive loyalty raises a question: Why? Why does God require this? Or to be more explicit, what gives God the right to demand exclusive worship of himself alone? Three reasons come to mind: the first is *legal*, the second is *love,* and the third is *pragmatic.*

The legal reason God has the right to demand unfettered loyalty is found in the statement just prior to the Ten Commandments:

> 2 I am the LORD your God, who brought you out of Egypt, out of the land of slavery
>
> Exodus 20:2

In other words, God's people throughout the ages have not merely discovered God by accident and decided to follow him because they reckoned it was a good idea. The people of God are able to enter into a relationship with him because he deliberately set about rescuing them from a horrible condition.

The original recipients of these Ten Commandments were recently slaves living under dreadful oppression and bondage. They were miserable and cried out to the Lord for mercy. God didn't have to do anything to help them. There was no obligation upon him to lift a finger, yet he did so. He went to huge lengths to rescue the Israelites from slavery and bondage to their Egyptian masters.

There is a particular legal concept associated with what God did for the Israelites: the concept of *redemption*. [6] In ancient cultures, the nature of slavery took different forms. Slavery in Egypt was different to slavery in later Greek and Roman cultures (and in other parts of the world throughout history), so it is contentious to speak of the conditions of slavery in uniform ways. Suffice it to say that generally, a slave had little to no status or rights. They were more like a chattel within a household, and with limits on their freedom. The usual way a slave changed the place where he or she lived was through a financial transaction; being redeemed or purchased by someone else, who became their new master. Here God is reminding the fledgling nation of that fact. They weren't running free from their Egyptian masters because of their own efforts or cunning. They were now no longer under bondage to their old masters because God had stepped in and redeemed them. In response to their cries for freedom, he had paid the purchase price for them. They were his people now and as their new legal owner, he had the right to dictate terms and conditions.

In other words, our relationship with God is not based on democratic principles nor is it a negotiated agreement or by mediation. It's more akin to the relationship of a slave toward his or her master. The one who has redeemed us or purchased our freedom from spiritual bondage and oppression (to our old sinful masters) has every right to demand our focus and loyalty and exclusive worship. Hence, the writer of Proverbs could say: "Fear of the Lord is the beginning of knowledge . . . " [7]

But lest we misunderstand the nature of God as our new legal owner, with the right to dictate our conduct, the second reason he requires our unfettered loyalty is his love and benevolence toward us.

6. Urdang and Flexner, "Redemption," p.1105
7. Proverbs 1:7

There is a wonderful story (possibly apocryphal but touching none the less) about Abraham Lincoln and a slave auction that he attended, prior to his election as President of the United States. It was well known that his public stance was for the abolition of slavery. He went to this slave auction only as an observer, but somehow became emotionally entangled as he watched a particularly tragic sight. A young black woman stood on the auction block, showing clear signs that she had been more than abused and taken advantage of by white men as slave owners in her past. Now she was being sold again. Lincoln could read the hatred, the hostility, and animosity that darted from her eyes and expression. And so, as the bidding went on he got caught up in it and entered a bid himself. In fact, he kept bidding until he won. Abraham Lincoln secured himself a slave! He went and arranged the necessary paperwork and after it was over he and the woman walked away together. Even though almost nothing was said between them he could feel her hatred and animosity. Finally, she turned to him and said,

"What are you going to do with me now?"

He said, "I'm going to set you free."

With no less animosity she said, "What do you mean free?"

He said, "Just free."

She said, "You mean free to say what I want to say."

"Free to say what you want to say," said Lincoln.

"Free to do what I want to do?"

"Free to do what you want to do."

"Free to go where I want to go?"

"Free to go where you want to go," said Lincoln.

Then she said in a different voice, "Then I'm going with you!"[8]

There is no question that God is our legal owner. The Bible says that all are enslaved by sin—no longer free; sin has become our master. As if each person stood on a metaphorical slave-traders auction block, having sold their soul to the highest bidder. Yet there was someone in the crowd who bid extra hard for us. The

8. Adapted from http://www.christianitytoday.com/moi/2000/001/january/lincoln-at-slave-block.html.

price was extremely high, but he was determined to win. His name is Jesus and the currency he paid was his own blood. Revelation 5:9 says of him:

> . . . with your blood you purchase men for God from every tribe and language and people and nation.

Our new owner loves us and wants the best for us. He is not interested in control or manipulation. He is not selfish or mean or cruel. He believes in us—to the extent that he gives us freedom of choice. He has the right to command loyalty and focus and worship, but he frees us to choose to do so of our own free will. The great, one, true God of Heaven and Earth makes himself vulnerable. He invites us to love him and to honor him with all our focus and energy. After all he has done to rescue us, and with all that he offers for those who choose to live for him, why wouldn't we choose to do that?

The third reason why God demands our exclusive loyalty is because he knows that when we give it to him, life works best for us. That's the theme picked up in Chapter 2 . . .

Small Group Discussion Questions

1. How necessary is it to have moral boundaries (rules) that govern personal behavior?

2. What would a society be like if there were no laws or rules to live by?

3. Many moral laws are determined these days by popular opinion (e.g. decriminalizing marijuana, lowering drinking age, euthanasia, etc.) What is a Christian response to lawmaking based upon majority opinion?

4. Do the Ten Commandments apply to Christians only, or to all people in the world?

5. The first commandment (no other gods) was given in an age when *polytheism* (many gods) was the norm. What are some of the (many) gods that people in our day and age worship?

6. In what way(s) has being a follower of Jesus limited your freedom of choice and behavior?

7. How would you explain a verse like Proverbs 1:7 to someone new or unfamiliar with Christianity?

8. What will you do differently in the coming week for considering the Ten Commandments?

Chapter 2

Honey, I Shrunk the Lord!

FOR MANY YEARS THE Disney Corporation ran a 3-D movie show at their Anaheim location called: *"Honey I Shrunk The Audience!"* Based on the 1989 movie, *"Honey, I Shrunk The Kids!,"* it featured a crazy nerd-scientist, Wayne Szalinski, who developed a machine that could shrink objects to 1/100th of their normal size. The title of the original movie was based upon a mishap with the machine, that shrunk the scientist's children, and the explanation of this unfortunate fact to his unsuspecting wife. The Disney theme park adaptation featured the scientist receiving an award for his incredible shrinking machine, but all went dreadfully wrong and the machine lurched in the direction of the audience, who were decked out with 3-D glasses. The audience's chairs moved, the room shook, compressed-air blew—simulating mice running across their feet—and with it the sensation of shrinking to a minute size. What looked like a 100-foot dog then appeared, in 3-D splendor right in front of the audience's faces and sneezed, at the same time little spits of water was released on the audience. *"Honey, I Shrunk The Audience!"* was a great ride.

In many respects, a sequel movie could well be made corresponding to the second of the Ten Commandments that God gave to Moses: *"Honey, I Shrunk The Lord!"*

The newly emerging nation of Israel had recently escaped the tyranny and oppression of their Egyptian masters. They found themselves in the desert, *en route* to a new land of promise, and God gave them ten value statements, or moral anchors, that would help them govern themselves. The first concerned their exclusive allegiance to God alone; the second followed on and focused on the issue of *idolatry*.

In this chapter, we explore what idolatry means and why it is forbidden. In short, it could be argued that the main issue has to do with shrinking or reformatting a deity to a size and shape that fits within our understanding:

> 4 You shall not make for yourself an image in the form of anything in heaven above or on the earth beneath or in the waters below. 5 You shall not bow down to them or worship them; for I, the LORD your God, am a jealous God, punishing the children for the sin of the parents to the third and fourth generation of those who hate me, 6 but showing love to a thousand generations of those who love me and keep my commandments.

Exodus 20:4–6

While not particularly central to the point of the text, over the years there have been differing opinions regarding the numbering of the Ten Commandments. There is universal agreement that the total number is ten, but some Christian communions, for example, the Catholics and Lutherans, regard verses 4–6 as part of the first commandment, rather than treating these verses separately as the second. That which other Protestants refer to as the tenth commandment, they divide into two parts: commandments nine and ten. Various reasons are given for the different numbering, but none of them detract from the point of the text. There are to be no other gods, and there is to be no worship of any *one*, or any *thing*, excepting the one true God of Heaven and Earth.

According to a quotation attributed to a seventh-century Puritan preacher, Thomas Wilson, "In the first commandment worshipping a false god is forbidden; in the second commandment worshipping the true God in a false manner is forbidden."

The main point to note is clear: God has very strong feelings about the issue of idolatry. This is not just the mellow advice of a parent to a child: "Please don't do that." The tone is more serious. It's more like, "I'm warning you, do that again and you are in very deep trouble!" God does not regard the sin of worshipping an idol as a little matter that can be brushed under the carpet or forgotten.

> 5 . . . I, the Lord your God, am a jealous God . . .

A word like *jealous* or *jealousy* is often employed today in a negative sense—describing a person who is resentful or envious of someone's possessions or position. Jealousy is frequently portrayed as a bad thing that most people don't like to admit to. However, this is not the meaning God intended to convey here. God doesn't indulge in resentment or experience pangs of envy.

The word *jealous* also means being intolerant of unfaithfulness and rivalry. A jealous husband or wife rightly expects the exclusive loyalty of their spouse. If a husband or wife has an affair with another person, it is not something which should be treated as trifling or insignificant. It hurts deeply and has the power to destroy the fabric of a marriage completely. Such is the intensity or fervor with which God jealously looks upon us and protects his right to be the sole focus of our worship.

The issue of idolatry, however, is about more than just hurting God's feelings. Bowing down or worshiping an idol, according to what God told Moses, carries a heavy-duty consequence. Not only will the unrepentant idol worshipper be punished, but so too will his or her offspring for three or four generations. The consequence for the crime of idol worship is particularly severe. To use a contemporary comparison, not only does the criminal who commits the crime go to jail, but so too do their children, their grandchildren, and their great-grandchildren!

Perhaps the severity of the consequence for idolatry begs an important question: *Why?* Why does God present himself as getting so hot and bothered over this issue? Why is it such a big deal? A number of suggestions have been put forward to explain why the act of idol worship might be so offensive to him.

As we have already noted in Chapter 1, to the original recipients these ten value statements represented a radical departure from the usual religious worldview of the day. This second commandment, in particular, represented a sharp and distinct separation from the religious practices in other, neighboring cultures. Being a follower of Yahweh, required that the nation demonstrate a visible difference in the way they conducted themselves and lived out their philosophy on life. Virtually every other religion in the world practiced idol worship. However, followers of Yahweh were to be distinctly different. There was to be a clear break with prevailing practices.

Might this be a principle that is as applicable today as it was 3500 years ago? When a person becomes a committed follower of Jesus Christ the language of *conversion* is often employed to describe their experience. A word like conversion implies change—an "about turn" with respect to attitude, priorities, and behavior. Christian conversion is much more than "adding God" to a person's existing life and portfolio of values. Instead, it signals a complete rearrangement of who they fundamentally are. To employ a domestic analogy, if a household converts from electricity to gas for heating or for cooking food they are obliged to replace old appliances with new ones. The new fuel simply won't work with old heaters, ovens or hot water cylinders. So too for the person who converts to Christianity: the old gods are discarded in favor of a new exclusive focus on the Lord.

Perhaps another reason why God pours so much scorn on idolatry is that it is just plain stupid or pointless. The prophet Isaiah offers a rather sarcastic portrayal of a man who cuts down a tree and then chops it up for three different purposes. From part of the tree he builds a fire to warm himself, and from another part he builds a fire to cook with and feed himself. From a third piece of the same wood he cuts and fashions an idol or figure of a god which he then bows down and worships, asking it to save him. [1] Isaiah's point is that this is ridiculous. How can a god you make with your own hands exercise power or good fortune over you?

1. Isaiah 44:13–17

Jeremiah similarly denounced the foolishness of idol worship:

> 3 For the customs of the peoples are worthless; they cut
> a tree out of the forest, and a craftsman shapes it with his
> chisel. 4 They adorn it with silver and gold; they fasten it
> with hammer and nails so it will not totter. 5 Like a scare-
> crow in a melon patch, their idols cannot speak; they
> must be carried because they cannot walk. Do not fear
> them; they can do no harm, nor can they do any good."

Jeremiah 10:3–5

Another major issue that God has with idols, we might say, is that in their essence they represent a breach of copyright. An idol is a fake, an illegitimate misrepresentation of the original. God cannot and will not be put in a box, or limited by the size of our imagination. As the copyright holder on himself, he will not allow his image to be copied, because no matter how much we try we can never capture him as he really is.

Perhaps it is like the holiday-maker who sees an amazing sight and seeks to record it with a photograph that they can look at or show to others. However, when looking at the captured image later, the photo doesn't seem to show the whole picture; maybe a piece is missing off the bottom outside the frame, or some of the definition isn't as clear as the original view. Likewise, the idol created or fashioned of God is at best a pathetic and incomplete misrepresentation of what he is really like. How can created beings ever describe or fashion an image of God that does him justice?

No doubt the major problem that God has with idols is that they inevitably distract people from genuine worship. To be fair, those who practice idol worship don't necessarily believe that the idol they bow down to, is actually their deity. Rather, the idol is a representation of a god, or an instrument of that god's power. For instance, in cultures within South and Central Asia images and figurines of their many deities adorn every wall, room, or taxi. These images are not perceived to be the god, rather these idols or pictures are a symbol or vehicle for focusing worship, a physical channel through which a homage can be paid, and the god's power dispensed.

And there may be some tempted to say, "What's so wrong with that?" After all the Bible says that God is invisible or spirit—unable to be seen or touched by way of human senses. Might not a picture or figurine representing him be a helpful prompt for our memory or a focus for our worship? The problem with idols is that the symbol tends to become the subject. That which begins as a prompt slowly and imperceptibly becomes the actual object of worship.

There is a good example of this in the life of the Israelites around the time the Ten Commandments were first given. A plague of venomous snakes attacked the Israelite community and many people died. When the Israelites called out to God for help, the Lord told Moses to make a bronze snake and put it on a pole. When people who were bitten by these snakes looked at the pole they were healed and lived on. The bronze snake on the pole was a symbol or reminder of God's ability to heal his chosen people.[2] The focus was clearly on God, and the snake was merely a signpost that pointed to him. However, the Israelite community apparently kept the effigy of the bronze snake. When Hezekiah became king of Judah, several hundred years later, the focus had changed. The people were offering incense to the snake and worshipping it as a god.[3] Hezekiah destroyed the symbol because it had usurped the place of God as the object of his people's worship.

This so often happens with the images of God that people create. People make idols to help them focus on God and remind them of their duty. Over time the object receives more attention than the one to whom it points. The focus is more and more concentrated on doing religious duty in front of the idol. Sacrifices are made to the replica or the image, and pure devotion to the god behind the idol becomes forgotten or neglected.

Consider as an analogy how an extramarital affair begins. Affairs don't usually happen overnight. Very few husbands and wives wake up one morning and decide, "Today I think I'll begin an affair!" No, it happens slowly and sometimes imperceptibly. A man

2. Numbers 21:8–9
3. 2 Kings 18:4

or women flirt a bit, and then a bit more, and then a bit more, and slowly the unique love they once had for their spouse is deflected, so that time, effort and devotion are eventually offered to a substitute lover. There are many occasions in the Old Testament where God uses the analogy of an extramarital affair to describe what his people do when they bow down to idols. Indeed, another description of idolatry in the Bible is spiritual adultery. True affection and worship of God are re-directed to a feeble replica or counterfeit deity. When God uses the term *jealous* he depicts himself as a person jilted by a lover, who has created and now bows down to an idol. Unsurprisingly, God is deeply offended.

Where does all this fit with our situation in the twenty-first century? Surely there isn't a lot of idol worship that goes on in nations founded on Judeo-Christian ethics? "Maybe there's a little bit amongst foreign immigrants, who come from idol-worshipping countries, but that isn't mainstream religious practice or our secular Western experience."

But is that actually the case? Perhaps religious objects and idol worship exists in our world today, unrecognized and called by other names? An example might be the fascination with new age religions or occultism that pervades Western cultures. Magazines, newspapers, websites, and television ads invite us to enjoy the mystical arts of fortune telling, horoscopes, tarot cards, and consultations with mediums. Investing in mystical crystals, reading a horoscope, having someone read our fortune in fun, or seeking to make contact with a loved one who has died, give credence to the influence of other spiritual realities and are an overt form of pagan worship. Sorcery and divination are expressly prohibited and is described in the Bible as an abomination in the eyes of the Lord. God specifically commands us to have nothing to do with such practices.[4]

Lest some may feel just a little smug that they don't partake in that kind of idol worship, remember that the apostle Paul also described greed as a form of idolatry:

---

4. Deuteronomy 18:10

5 Put to death, therefore, whatever belongs to your earthly nature: sexual immorality, impurity, lust, evil desires and greed, which is idolatry

Colossians 3:5

According to the Bible, an insatiable hunger for the gratification of personal appetites and the endless pursuit of more possessions is pure idolatry. The opposite of greed is contentment—being happy with what we have and resting on the Lord as our provider. The constant want for more is an act of idolatry to an illegitimate lover. This theme is elaborated upon in Chapter 10.

Perhaps another insidious form of idolatry might be the image that people develop of what God is really like. Here we come back to our theme of: *"Honey, I shrunk the Lord!"* God is reduced to the measure of our perception, our cultural values, or our capacity for understanding. Whereas God is so much bigger than our image of him.

In the first chapter of the Bible we read that God created humankind in his own image; male and female we are created in the image of God! Sometimes we can be guilty of reversing the created order and making or imagining God in our own image. We form God, according to our perception of what he *should* be, after our image—or at least our imagination. For example, the person who said, "I can believe in a God of love who invites people to live forever in Heaven, but I cannot believe in a God who allows people to go to Hell. My God wouldn't do that!" What they are really saying is: *"I wouldn't do that!"* Might the image of God they worship be more attuned to their perception of how a God should behave than what the Bible actually teaches?

Making or imagining God as being like us is undoubtedly a form of idolatry. In contemporary churches, it can occur as people critique modes and idioms of worship music. They assume that God has the same musical taste as they do. Like the man who complained to a friend after a church service, "I got absolutely nothing out of that hour of worship!" To which his friend wisely replied, "That's interesting—I didn't realize we were worshipping you!" In reality, God is so much bigger, broader and more complex than our mental snapshot of him.

Most of the Jewish people in Jesus' day missed the coming of the Messiah because the image they held of God was a few degrees askew. Their perception of God may not have been made of bronze or wood, but in their minds it was certainly concrete! Unfortunately, it was also inadequate. The Messiah came to his own people and his own people "received him not."[5] They didn't even recognize him.

Another form of idolatry might be the priority some traditions, objects, symbols, and behavior have had in prescribing our approach to worship. For some people, a church isn't a church unless it has a cross or a baptismal pool. "And if we have one it ought to be at the center of our auditorium, not off to one side." For some people, a place of worship should be sacrosanct and sealed off for that purpose only. God's house shouldn't be used for anything else but worship.

To offer a personal example, one of our children was married in a different church, hiring it because they loved the look of the building. At the wedding rehearsal the night before, some of the little children belonging to wedding party members ran around the pews and up and down the aisles laughing and having fun. That is, until the priest of the parish walked in and shouted at them to stop at the top of his voice, asserting that the "sanctuary" was holy and to be a place of prayer, not a playground for children! It could be argued that his theological paradigm of Jesus completely missed the point. Might it not be imagined that Jesus was running around and playing with the little children—making God's house a place of fun!

Then there are the musical instruments that are played in church—surely these should only be those that will be used in Heaven, right, organs and pianos? And the King James version of the Bible is the only one we should read from in church (. . . after all, if it was good enough for the Apostle Paul its good enough for us!). Oh, and the old hymn books offer real anthems for worship,

5. John 1:11

that God truly likes, and are so much more appropriate than the modern rubbish!

When we give excess honor and power to things like this, aren't we creating idols for ourselves to worship? The "thing" takes the focus of our attention from the Lord. The heart of our worship becomes distracted as we focus on the idols.

Perhaps another way we practice idolatry is the devotion we give to the events that clutter up our lives. Or as one commentator put it, "A man's god is that which he thinks to be the most important thing in his life." The word *worship* simply means worth-ship. It means giving of honor, reverence, and prestige to that which we regard as being valuable or important. Worship might be described as that which grabs and holds our attention and absorbs our energy. For some people, a car is an idol that they worship and polish and adore. For some, it might be education, a career, or chasing after promotion. That which drives them and consumes their focus is their worth. There is no room for anything else apart from the idol. Some people worship their house, their television set, cell phone, or even their social life or family.

Jesus once got into a conversation with a wealthy young man about the meaning of life, and after talking with him for a while identified the idol that prevented him from receiving eternal life. The young man evidently valued his wealth above all else, and Jesus' advice to him was to destroy this idol, depriving it of its influence and power, by giving it away to the poor.[6]

The point of the first and second commandment is that God will not share the allegiance he is owed with any "one" or any "thing" else. If he is to be our God, he must have our total attention. No other gods and no other images, idols or symbols that might distract from our devotion to him can be permitted.

In closing this chapter, we return to a point foreshadowed at the end of the first chapter. One of the reasons God demands our exclusive loyalty is because he knows that when we yield to him, life works best for us. In other words, there is a pragmatic reason for having no other gods or idols. In Matthew 6, Jesus spoke about

---

6. Luke 18:22

the pressure and struggles people experience. There is much in our everyday existence that causes worry or fretting and anxiety. Jesus makes this statement:

> 33 But seek first his kingdom and his righteousness, and all these things will be given to you as well . . .

The essence of what Jesus was saying, in this part of his famous sermon on a Galilean hillside, was that when we put God first, or at the center of our lives, all the other pressures and anxieties of life come into balance. When we eliminate other gods and distracting idols, making God our primary focus, the rest of life makes sense. We benefit when we align ourselves with the divine order and a God who is willing and able to guide us through the maze of daily living and provide all our needs.

There is no denying the fact that the Christian faith is exclusive. You cannot mix oil with water. Christianity does not tolerate other religions or their practices. It is all of God, or it is none of him. However, for those who give him everything and make him the exclusive focus of their worship, life works.

Small Group Discussion Questions

1. Immigration policies in recent decades have resulted in many different religions finding expression in countries with strong Judeo-Christian heritage, and with them varying forms of idol worship. What do you consider to be a Christian response to this?

2. Why do you think God is so strong (hot!) over the issue of idol worship?

3. What are some of the subtle (less obvious) idols that people bow down to and worship?

4. How would you explain God's *jealousy* (Exodus 20:5) to someone who wasn't a Christian?

5. God's punishment of idol worship transfers down generational lines (Exodus 20:5). How would you respond to the person who says this isn't fair?

6. When we repent (turn away) from our sin God forgives us completely (1 John 1:9), and this must apply to the children and grandchildren of repentant idol worshippers. How does a person go about repenting of idol worship in their family line?

7. How will consideration of this second commandment affect your life in the week ahead?

Chapter 3

What's in a Name?

ON 7TH FEBRUARY 1996, a tragedy occurred in Hillsborough County, in the State of Florida. Three teenagers died in a car accident, as a result of driving through an intersection into the path of an eight-ton truck. During an investigation into the cause of the accident, the police found that a "Stop" sign had been pulled out of the ground and was lying on the side of the road beside the intersection. It turned out that another group of young people, the previous night, thought it was fun to go around Hillsborough County stealing or knocking over road signs at traffic intersections. Further investigation led to the names of the young people responsible; they were arrested, eventually convicted of manslaughter, and received hefty jail terms. In sentencing them the judge made the comment, "I don't believe for one moment that you pulled up those signs with the intent of causing the death of anyone, but pulling up the signs caused ramifications that none of you may have expected."[1]

Welcome to the world in which we live, where the rules are constantly changing. The intersections of life are littered with uprooted road signs lying on the ground. Where there used to be a moral "Stop" sign, now there is often nothing warning us to slow down or to proceed with caution.

1. New York Times, 1997/06/21

Some people call a world without rules, *freedom*. They argue that the inhibiting shackles of old-fashioned morality have fallen off and we are now freer to do what we feel like doing without any sense of guilt. The reality, however, is that the removal of moral road signs makes the intersections of life very insecure and dangerous places. "For lack of a warning, will my free choice lead me unknowingly into the path of an eight-ton truck?"

As we noted in Chapter 1, some question the relevance of the 3500-year-old values from an ancient culture to a supposedly more enlightened twenty-first century. "Do we really need these Ten Commandments? After all, they're old-fashioned and inhibiting; they conflict with our twenty-first-century worldview."

Yet isn't it interesting that as society drifts away from its roots and destroys or disregards the traditional values that God offered his people, the result seems to be greater moral carnage. Nations and cultures turn their back on God's foundational values and then wonder why there is:

- more crime
- more divorce
- more drug abuse
- more alcoholism
- more suicide
- more people in prison
- more home invasions
- more violence
- more murder
- more sexual perversion
- more single-parents.

The first two commandments are about making and keeping God as the unrivaled center of our lives and our worldview; the third is about not treating God with contempt or flippancy:

7 You shall not misuse the name of the LORD your God,
for the LORD will not hold anyone guiltless who misuses
his name.

Exodus 20:7

The first question to be asked of this verse is what *"misuse the
name of the Lord"* really means, or as some English Bibles translate
it: *"take the name of the Lord in vain?"*

On face value, this commandment could be misunderstood,
depicting God as having an overly sensitive disposition; as someone who doesn't like having his name ridiculed or made fun of. As
if God might benefit from a recital of the playground rhyme that
many grew up with, "Sticks and stones will break my bones, but
names will never hurt me." In other words, it doesn't really matter
what we're called, because name-calling is insignificant, it doesn't
affect people. (Of course, in more recent years the wisdom of this
response to taunting has come into question; actually, the names
people are called does cause hurt, and can do significant damage—
but that is a subject for another time.)

However, the third commandment has more substance to
it than this. In ancient Hebrew thinking, as in other cultures, the
name given to a person was extremely significant. It meant more
than a *handle* or a way of distinguishing one person from another.
A name had meaning, significance or symbolism, and was believed
to have an influence on the way that person matured or developed.
As a child grew up the expectation was that they would grow into
the likeness depicted by their name. Sometimes if a person's character or reputation changed, the name by which they were known
also changed. Take Jacob, for example, who had his name changed
to Israel. Saul, the former persecutor of Christians, became known
as Paul. When the disciple Simon met Jesus, Jesus evidently saw
future strength and dependability within him and his name was
changed to Peter, meaning "rock."

We often make associations because of a name. It conjures up
a picture in our mind and sometimes even a physical reaction in
our body. For instance, if names such as Adolph Hitler or Osama
Bin Laden are spoken in our hearing a mental image is formed.

Or if the name of a famous fashion model was mentioned, a different image might be formed in the minds of the ladies than in the minds of the men. The women might see someone skinny and possibly anorexic, whereas the men might see a picture of . . . well, probably best we don't go there!

The name of a person is imbued with their reputation or image. If we were to apply for a job and were asked to submit references from people who could vouch for our integrity and honesty, submitting a reference from our mother probably wouldn't carry the same influence with a prospective employer as one from a well-known person or someone with particular experience in the field within which we want to work. If a person with a credible reputation vouches for us, their name carries weight.

When it comes to God, throughout the Bible there are numerous references and metaphors for "the name of the Lord." For instance, Proverbs 18:10 states, "The name of the Lord is a strong tower; the righteous run to it and are safe." Or Psalm 20:1 encourages us, "May the Lord answer you when you are in distress; may the name of the God of Jacob protect you." These aren't references to a particular title for God; they refer to his character or reputation. God has shown himself to be a refuge and a strong protector whom people can rely upon.

At the end of World War I, Herbert Hoover was responsible for relief efforts in Europe on behalf of the Allied Forces. We know more about him as someone later elected to be the thirty-first President of the United States, but his early reputation or name was linked with effective rehabilitation work in war-torn European cities. Hundreds of thousands of people were literally saved from starvation as a result of the work he did. His name became synonymous with humanitarian aid—so much so that a new word entered the Finnish language. In Finnish to "hoover" means to "be kind or to help." [2] Herbert Hoover's name was conjoined with his reputation. To be known by a certain name, or to have the name of

---

2. Cornell College, "*The Great Humanitarian, Herbert Hoover's Food Relief Efforts*," http://www.cornellcollege.edu/history/courses/stewart/his260-3-2006/01%20one/fin.htm

someone influential behind you, opens doors that might otherwise stay closed.

How then is the third Commandment broken? What does it actually mean to "misuse the name of the Lord" or to "take it in vain?"

In the original Hebrew language of the Ten Commandments, the word translated as "misuse" or "take in vain" meant "empty; treat as insincere; frivolous or idle." It implied the making of something devoid of any truth or real significance. [3] Therefore, to misuse the name of the Lord is to regard or treat it as unimportant, as having no value or worth. The second half of this commandment states that this is a really serious thing to do:

> ... the LORD will not hold anyone guiltless who misuses the name of the LORD.

Treating the name of God with contempt, using it inappropriately, or being flippant with God's honor and reputation, is not a small matter. There will come a day of reckoning for those who misuse the name of the Lord.

Once again, how do people do this? Surely, *we* don't do this, right?

Maybe we might, without realizing it. Perhaps one of the more blatant ways that the third commandment is broken today is with profanity. The word "God" or "Jesus," or "Christ," or "Lord" frequently occurs in conversation today, but in most cases, it's used as an expletive!

There is a story of a little girl, named Mary, who attended Sunday School for the first time just before Christmas. She eagerly listened as the teacher told of the birth of God's Son. She was enthralled with the story of the angels and the wise men and the gifts and the star, and then the teacher added, "and they called him Jesus." Mary turned to the person beside her with a puzzled look on her face, "Why did they name such a sweet little baby with a swear word?" It was the first time she had ever heard this name used other than as a curse!

---

3. Barclay, William, *The Ten Commandments*, p.13

So, one way of understanding the third commandment could be as a declaration that use of a reference to God as an expletive is out-of-bounds. It's wrong or blasphemy. It's an offense against the Lord to use a reference to God as a means of making a point, expressing surprise, or reinforcing anger. When was the last time we heard a person stub their toe, or hit their finger with a hammer, and then cry out: "O Buddha!" or "O Allah!" Yet just about every day people are heard expressing surprise, or underscoring their opinion, with words like "O God yes!" or "Jesus Christ!" . . . and not in the context of a prayer!

There is a lot of emphasis today around what a person eats or consumes. We are warned off consuming products that will spoil our bodies or corrupt our physiology. In Matthew 15 Jesus made an interesting comment along these lines:

> 11 What goes into someone's mouth does not defile them, but what comes out of their mouth, that is what defiles them.

Matthew 15:11

Paying a little more attention to what comes out of a person's mouth might mean we fare better in the long run. Those who follow Jesus must learn to keep a tight rein on their tongue. Sometimes that means having to learn a whole new vocabulary. After the Welsh revivals in the early years of the twentieth century, where many foul-mouthed miners were converted, there were stories of mules (which were used to pull carts of coal) needing to be retrained. The animals were unable to understand the commands of their newly-converted masters since they no longer swore at them. Or in another instance, a farmer arrived home much later than his wife expected him. When asked what took him so long, he replied, "Well, I picked up the Reverend down the road and gave him a lift home, and from that moment on the horses didn't seem to understand a thing I said to them!"

If misusing the name of God as a swear word or an expletive has been a part of our practice, resolve today to stop doing so.

Lest we might think we have this commandment covered because we don't use foul language, the main issue with misusing the name of the Lord probably isn't about swearing. The bigger issue is about people who misrepresent or misappropriate their connection with God. The Bible says that not only is the name of the Lord an expression of his own character and faithfulness, it also maintains that God has made the power of his name and reputation available to his children. On numerous occasions, we have been given authority to use the name of the Lord. To employ a contemporary analogy, it might be as if God has said to his followers, "Here, take my credit card, and if you find something you need, charge it to my account."

For instance, Jesus said:

> You may ask me for anything in my name and I will do it . . .
>
> John 14:13–14

> In my name they will drive out demons . . .
>
> Mark 16:17

> In my name they will lay hands on the sick and they will be healed
>
> Mark 16:18

The Apostle Paul used the metaphor similarly:

> Everyone who calls on the name of the LORD will be saved . . .
>
> Romans 10:13

> We are justified in the name of the LORD . . .
>
> 1 Corinthians 6:11

> At the name of Jesus every knee will bow . . .
>
> Philippians 2:10

God has lent us his reputation or his divine (purchasing) power. In Ephesians 1:5, Paul states that God has adopted us into his family, whereby we now have access to all the glorious riches of his heavenly realm. This is a particularly powerful personal analogy for our family. When our daughter Sarah was born she didn't have a family name. In the Bangladesh orphanage where she spent her first six months, she was simply known as *Ruby*. However, when my wife and I adopted her, she became part of our family and she received our family name. She was no longer a nobody; she had an identity and a history. She now appears on my family tree. Because of my name, which is now her name, the government of New Zealand recognized and granted her citizenship, as if she was born in our country, with all the rights and privileges that go with that identity.

In the same way, when God offers the people of our world the privilege of calling him "Lord," we become sons and daughters of the Most High God; heirs of the King of Kings and Lord of Lords; adopted into his family. However, with the privilege comes the responsibility, the challenge to live up to this new family name. Careless conduct or careless speech can discredit not just ourselves, but also the reputation of the Christian family and its name.

A major implication of applying the teaching of the third Commandment to our lives is the necessity of examining our conduct. This goes beyond merely using God's name incorrectly, it also includes misrepresentation of a person's connection with him. From time to time an audit of our behavior and the asking of tough questions regarding our relationship is appropriate, "Is my Christian commitment or connection with God reflecting a positive image to those around me, or do I bring discredit to the one I represent and whose name I bear?"

Over the years the integrity of the British singer, Sir Cliff Richard, as a deeply committed follower of Jesus, has been impressive. For years, the media hounded him to see if his lifestyle matched his Christian profession. This is why recent accusations of inappropriate behavior, though eventually proven to be baseless, were so devastating. Cliff Richard once described his reputation in these terms: "What people think of me is becoming less and less important; what they think of Jesus because of me is critical."[4]

In Romans 2, Paul wrote about his Jewish peers, those who supposedly knew God and understood his word but who lived hypocritical lives. He suggested that their hypocrisy or double standards were a form of blasphemy and a major source of people losing interest in God:

> 24 As it is written: "God's name is blasphemed among the Gentiles because of you."

When Christians behave in ways that conflict with our family reputation they defame the name of the Lord. In Titus 1:16, Paul described hypocrisy in these terms:

> 16 They claim to know God, but by their actions they deny him. They are detestable, disobedient and unfit for doing anything good.

It could be argued that the people for whom the third Commandment is primarily recorded were not unbelievers, who blasphemed and used God's name as a swear word. In their ignorance, they might not have known any better. Or, the real challenge may have been to those who claimed to know God. Did their lifestyle match the character and power and love of God with whom they claimed a relationship? Indeed, it's been suggested that "the hypocrisy of the church is far worse than the profanity of the street."[5] Think about what might offend God more; the fact that people use his name as a swear word, or that people who claim to worship and follow him, live an inappropriate lifestyle in front of others?

The Apostle Peter wrote to the Christians of his day with a challenge to the integrity of the life they led and its impact on those who witnessed it:

> 11 Dear friends, I urge you, as foreigners and exiles, to abstain from sinful desires, which wage war against your soul. 12 Live such good lives among the pagans that,

---

4. Richard, Cliff, *AZ Qoutes*, quote/823776
5. Laurie, Greg, *The Christian Post*

though they accuse you of doing wrong, they may see your good deeds and glorify God on the day he visits us.

1 Peter 2:11–12

To employ the language of citizenship and patriotic loyalty, followers of Jesus no longer belong to this world. Their real home is with God in Heaven. Their citizenship has been changed. They are aliens and exiles in this world. Or to use another analogy, Christians are in diplomatic service amongst the people of this world. Others watch what they say or do; everything about them is scrutinized and viewed as a reflection of the government and nation they represent.

To hammer this home still further, consider the people among whom we live—our neighbors, next door or across the street. Most probably they have a fair idea where we go each week for worship. They've probably noticed us when we get into our car on a Sunday morning wearing nice clothes. They have figured out that we attend a church for the purpose of worship. They may, or may not, have much understanding about the Christian faith, but chances are they know that the name of God rolls off the lips of Christians in praise and thanksgiving. They possibly won't ever say so to us directly, but we're being watched, and so is our connection with God. How might the veracity of our God-connection be measured? Is it what we are when we are gathered with other believers in a church building once a week, or is it how we behave on the other six days of the week?

- Do we keep our word?
- Are we polite and winsome in our dealings with people?
- Do we show respect for the property of others?
- Does the language of our mouth match our profession of faith?
- Are we honest?
- Do we pay our bills . . . on time?
- Is our temper under control?

- Are we punctual, honest and diligent at work?

- Do we demonstrate kingdom values in how we manage and spend our money?

God has made available to his followers, his chosen people on Earth, the full extent of his grace and power. Believers have God's credit card, as it were; and may use the authority of his name to open doors. But we also have a responsibility, a family reputation to uphold.

The challenge of the third Commandment is that we use his name with honor. Why? Because people are around us, and they are watching!

Small Group Discussion Questions

1. How do you feel about your name? If you could have any other name in the world what would it be?

2. How would you explain a verse like Proverbs 18:10 to someone new or unacquainted with the Christian faith?

3. The third commandment condemns the use of God's titles as swear words. What about other words? Who (or how) should decide what is acceptable language and what isn't?

4. How does Jesus' statement in Matthew 15:11 challenge you?

5. Ephesians 1:5 says that we have been adopted into God's family; we now bear his name. What difference does that make in how you live?

6. What are some of the ways Christians put people off Christianity?

7. 1 Peter 2:11,12 says that Christians are different. How do we demonstrate our difference?

8. What will you do differently this coming week for considering the third commandment?

Chapter 4

The Law of Self Maintenance

A PASTOR ATTENDED A Pastors' conference one weekend. On the Sunday morning, he decided to play a round of golf instead of attending the conference church service. He felt somewhat guilty doing this on the Lord's Day when his congregation would be gathering for worship and he recalled that several of his sermons had been about breaking the Sabbath. In the end, however, he figured no one from back home would know what he was doing, so off to the course he went. He stood on the first tee and took a practice swing. Again, pangs of guilt began to flood through his mind, "Shouldn't I be in church rather than out here on the golf course?"

Unbeknown to the pastor a couple of angels were sitting in a tree down the fairway watching what was going on. The junior angel said to the senior angel, "What are we going to do? Should I do something that teaches him a lesson? Perhaps he could trip in the ditch and break his leg?"

The senior angel replied, "No, no. I have a better idea. Watch this!" As the pastor raised his club for his first tee-shot the angel got behind the swing and gave it a bit of heavenly assistance. It was unquestionably the best drive the pastor had ever made! The ball sailed high and straight, landing on the green three meters short of the pin, and then gently rolled right into the cup for a hole-in-one!

The junior angel said to the senior angel, "What did you do that for? How is that going to teach him a lesson?"

The senior angel replied, "Yes it was a great shot . . . but who is this guy ever going to be able to tell considering when and where it happened!"

The fourth of the Ten Commandments God gave to the newly emerging nation of Israel was all about a day for worship and rest:

> 8 Remember the Sabbath day by keeping it holy. 9 Six days you shall labor and do all your work, 10 but the seventh day is a sabbath to the LORD your God. On it you shall not do any work, neither you, nor your son or daughter, nor your male or female servant, nor your animals, nor any foreigner residing in your towns. 11 For in six days the LORD made the heavens and the earth, the sea, and all that is in them, but he rested on the seventh day. Therefore, the LORD blessed the Sabbath day and made it holy.
>
> Exodus 20:8–11

Of all the Ten Commandments, arguably this one has attracted the most controversy over the years. A range of views have been put forward as to how this commandment fits within our twenty-first-century context. With reference to the meaning of the word there is agreement, "sabbath" literally means to "desist," "cease," or "rest from what you are doing." It refers to the stopping or curtailing of one's normal activity. However, just how the principle of sabbath-rest is to be applied has been the subject of various interpretations.

There are some who say this was an instruction for the Jewish nation and religion, and it doesn't necessarily cross over into the New Testament or the era of Christianity. The sabbath-rest is likened to some of the ancient ceremonial and dietary laws that Moses recorded which have been superseded by the "new covenant." These practices should, therefore, be regarded as relics from the past which are irrelevant today. On the other side of the coin, there are some branches of the Christian church who adamantly insist that the literal Sabbath, as in the seventh day of the week, ought to be observed by Christians as it was for Jews. Saturday is the day we should gather for worship, rather than Sunday.

Some of the most ardent arguments for maintaining, or perhaps reclaiming, the literal Sabbath day fall into what some have called the "weird and wonderful" category—possibly more "weird" than "wonderful!" These can be confusing for those with little understanding of Church history. Many books have been written asserting that Saturday is the correct day for observing the Sabbath and implying that if we truly love God and obey the Scriptures we will gather for worship on this day. This, they argue, was the model Jesus followed, and it is to this that the majority of believers worshipping in contemporary churches need to return.

Some have also asserted that the shifting of the Christian Sabbath from Saturday to Sunday dates from a ruling given by the newly converted Emperor Constantine and was one of his many corruptions of original Christian faith and practice. Actually, there is ample reference to New Testament Christians observing Sunday as their day of worship, commemorating the day of Jesus' resurrection, hundreds of years before Constantine.[1]

Then there are some Christians who argue that the principle of sabbath-rest applies primarily to recreation and leisure activities that interrupt a busy work schedule. Others suggest that this passage in Exodus 20 focuses only on worship and honoring God, and so every day ought to be a "sabbath" for Christians.

There is the whole social debate of recent decades regarding Sunday trading. As Western societies become increasingly secular and shake off the shackles of their religious foundation, should retail outlets, for instance, be permitted to open on the Lord's day or on religious holy days like Easter or Christmas? Some have contended that nations bring themselves under a curse because their contemporary laws permit shops to open and trade on the Sabbath. This raises the question of whether this is a moral issue that the Church should take a stand on for the sake of society as a

---

1 Cf. Acts 20:7; 1 Corinthians 16:2. (See also references to the initial evidence of the day of the resurrection: Matthew 28:1; Mark 16:2; Mark 16:9; Luke 24:1; John 20:1; John 20:19.)

whole, or whether it is just a principle Christians should apply to themselves.

Another related issue is permissible behavior on the Sabbath. If work is prohibited, what about sport? Many Christians alive today grew up in homes where sport on a Sunday (including playing cards and board games!), was absolutely forbidden. Over the years, famous Christian personalities have refused to play sport on a Sunday because of their interpretation of the Sabbath. In contrast, other equally committed Christian sportsmen and sportswomen have held a different view and were willing to play on Sundays.

One thing we know for certain is that controversy surrounding the interpretation and application of biblical teaching on sabbath-rest is not new to our day and age. It has been a bone of contention for thousands of years. Stepping back to the era when the Ten Commandments were first given, there's an example in Numbers 15 of how seriously they took the idea of Sabbath-keeping. A certain Israelite took the prohibition a bit lightly and was caught outside the camp gathering firewood on the Sabbath. He was brought before Moses and Aaron who, it would seem, weren't sure how to deal with him. Apparently, as Moses pondered what to do the Lord gave him this piece of advice:

> 35 Then the LORD said to Moses, "The man must die. The whole assembly must stone him outside the camp."

Numbers 15:35

During the intertestamental period, prior to the time of Jesus, it was a serious issue that exercised the minds of the Jewish legal fraternity. It was one thing for God to forbid work on the Sabbath, but such a prohibition was deemed unhelpful because it lacked specificity. For example, what constitutes the nature of work? This may sound bizarre in our contemporary age, but a few hundred years prior to the time of Jesus, Jewish scholars identified and documented a list of 1521 things that were not permissible on the Sabbath. For example, you could not rescue a drowning person on the Sabbath. Untying knots that only needed one hand was permissible, but if two hands were required it was forbidden.

If a man's ox fell into the ditch he could pull it out, but if the man fell in himself he had to stay there until the Sabbath concluded. You could take a sip of vinegar for food, but if you took a sip of vinegar to help an aching tooth this was considered to have broken the Sabbath. If a man was bitten by a flea on the Sabbath he had to allow the flea to keep on biting him, for if he tried to stop the flea from biting, or if he killed it, he was guilty of hunting on the Sabbath!

Another class of work that was forbidden was the carrying of a burden. That raised the question of what constituted a burden? Was it permissible to carry a child on the Sabbath? The answer was "yes," provided the child didn't have a stone in his hand, for a stone was deemed a burden.[2] Likewise, if you worked as a tailor, you needed to check you didn't have a needle stuck in your clothing on the Sabbath, since sewing was forbidden.[3] If a man dragged his chair on the ground, and inadvertently caused a furrow in the soil with the legs of the chair, was he guilty of plowing on the Sabbath? Even today in some hotels in Israel where the devout and orthodox stay there are such things as *Sabbath lifts*, which automatically stop at every floor in the building so that people traveling up to their room don't have to "work" the lift on the Sabbath.[4]

When it came to illness or injury, it was deemed permissible for a Jew to take steps to stop a person from getting worse, however any effort to cure him or make him better was deemed out of bounds on the Sabbath. Hence the consternation Jesus caused when he healed people on the Sabbath.

If all of this sounds a bit strange and primitive, there are similar stories of legalism a little closer to our day and age. In Scotland, in the seventeenth century, there was a famous case of a man arrested and brought before the court for the crime of smiling on a Sunday!

Another, perhaps humorous, anecdote dates back to 1849 when Zachary Taylor was elected as the twelfth President of the

2. Barclay, William, *The Ten Commandments*, p.18
3. Barclay, William, *The Gospel of Matthew Vol. 1*, p128.
4. Warner, Rob, *The Ten Commandments and the Decline of the West*, p 70.

United States. As a deeply devout man, he refused to be inaugurated on the proposed date which was a Sunday. Fellow politicians pleaded with him to change his mind, but because of his strong religious convictions, he stood his ground. This apparently created a constitutional crisis as the US Constitution forbade the former president, James K. Polk, remaining in office an extra day beyond the conclusion of his term. The US Senate had to appoint an interim-president from noon on Sunday 4th March through to noon on Monday 5th March, when Zachary Taylor agreed to assume executive office. The man appointed was Senator David Rice Atchison. Unfortunately, during the week leading up to the Senator assuming office for twenty-four hours, his life had been extremely hectic. He retired to bed late on the Saturday night having instructed his landlady not to wake him for any reason. She followed his orders to the letter and Senator Atchison slept through Sunday and on into Monday, past the time at which his 24-hour interim period as President concluded. He is notably the only US president on record to have slept through his entire term of office!

When we consider the example and teaching of Jesus we're bound to draw the conclusion that there has been considerable "missing of the point" when it comes to Sabbath-keeping. On at least two occasions Jesus himself encountered controversy over allegedly doing the wrong thing on the Lord's day. In Luke 13 there is the account of Jesus healing a woman at a synagogue and being rebuked in response by the ruler of the synagogue:

> 14 Indignant because Jesus had healed on the Sabbath, the synagogue ruler said to the people, "There are six days for work. So come and be healed on those days, not on the Sabbath." 15 The LORD answered him, "You hypocrites! Doesn't each of you on the Sabbath untie his ox or donkey from the stall and lead it out to give it water? 16 Then should not this woman, a daughter of Abraham, whom Satan has kept bound for eighteen long years, be set free on the Sabbath day from what bound her?" 17 When he said this, all his opponents were humiliated, but the people were delighted with all the wonderful things he was doing.
>
> Luke 13: 14–17

The other occasion is even more significant because in response to it Jesus gives a very clear statement about how we should understand the principle of sabbath-rest:

> 23 One Sabbath Jesus was going through the grain fields, and as his disciples walked along, they began to pick some heads of grain. 24 The Pharisees said to him, "Look, why are they doing what is unlawful on the Sabbath?" 25 He answered, "Have you never read what David did when he and his companions were hungry and in need? 26 In the days of Abiathar the high priest, he entered the house of God and ate the consecrated bread, which is lawful only for priests to eat. And he also gave some to his companions."
>
> 27 Then he said to them, "The Sabbath was made for man, not man for the Sabbath. 28 So the Son of Man is LORD even of the Sabbath."
>
> Mark 2:23–28

Clearly, Jesus pulled the rug out from under many of the legalistic interpretations and applications of Sabbath observance. The purpose of the Sabbath is to bless, not to hinder us. It is something for us, not something against us.

Looking at this fourth commandment through the lens of Jesus, if the Sabbath is made for man, not man for the Sabbath, what therefore is its point? What is the value-added or benefit associated with sabbath-rest? Two key principles are worth considering:

1. Balance in lifestyle

One way of applying the teaching of the fourth commandment might be the old saying: "All work and no play makes Jack a dull boy." In God's wisdom and order, people ought not to work continuously without a break. The pattern God set for us in creation is six days on, one day off.

> 11 For in six days the LORD made the heavens and the earth, the sea, and all that is in them, but he rested on the

seventh day. Therefore, the LORD blessed the Sabbath day
and made it holy.

Exodus 20:8–11

That's not to suggest that God took a holiday or went fishing
on the Sabbath, because he got exhausted from all that creation
work. The God of the Bible neither slumbers nor sleeps. God was
merely setting an example or giving us a standard to live by, which
is certainly how the writer of Hebrews 4:9–11 described God's
intent.

> 9 There remains, then, a Sabbath-rest for the people of
> God; 10 for anyone who enters God's rest also rests from
> their works, just as God did from his. 11 Let us, there-
> fore, make every effort to enter that rest, so that no one
> will perish by following their example of disobedience.

In short, it is not wise or healthy for a person to work seven
days a week, 52 weeks of the year. We might want to say that the
person who does so challenges God's wisdom and is saying that
they are better or more capable than he is!

There is an old Greek proverb: "The bow that is always bent
(so that the string is always stretched taut) will soon cease to shoot
straight." The person who is frenetically busy 24/7 invariably burns
out. A health-fuse will blow.

A taxi driver was asked how many miles he expected to get
out of his taxi. He said he had driven his previous vehicle for over
250,000 miles without a single major engine repair and that he
fully expected to do the same thing with his current taxi. When
asked how he could possibly put that many kilometers onto a car
he replied with a single word, "*Maintenance*."

Indeed, the fourth commandment could well be summed up
as the principle of personal maintenance. Sometimes we need to
take our car off the road and spend a bit of money on it in order to
lengthen its lifespan. The principle behind sabbath-rest or taking a
break can be likened to preventative maintenance. Stopping work,
relaxing, or engaging in a hobby, is wise advice that comes from
the very example of God himself.

Actually, the fourth commandment also has a Human Resources (HR) implication for those who employ or oversee people in the workplace. The principle wasn't applied just to bosses or self-employed people, but also to employees, children, and even to slaves:

> . . . on it you should not do any work, neither you, nor your son or daughter, nor your manservant or maidservant, nor your animals, nor the alien within your gates.

The fourth commandment is a challenge to those who lead or employ others. Is too much expected from employees? If we are a boss, are those who work for us able to exercise wisdom in how they care for themselves? The fourth commandment speaks to industrial relations and how employers treat their employees. All work and no play is a form of exploitation.

On the one hand, the Bible teaches against being lazy—laziness or being slothful is specifically spoken of as a sin. On the other hand, those who work too hard and too long are considered equally guilty. To burn-out is not much better than rusting out. Maybe there's a challenge to stop and ponder here. Is our life in balance? Is our work life sufficiently punctuated with "sabbath breaks?" Or are we pushing ourselves beyond reasonable limits? Do we work to live, or are we living to work?

Of course, this principle of sabbath-rest doesn't only apply to people in paid employment. It also applies to the frenetic pace we live life in general. Consider this statement from Rob Warner's book, "*The Ten Commandments and the Decline of the West*,"

> "Life is getting faster in the western world. People are finding it more and more difficult to take time to relax. Children have been sucked into this culture of relentless achievement. There was a time when children would simply play together after school. Now middle-class parents rush them from a music class to a sports experience and then to a personal tutor, paying for a different organized activity every night of the week. We are turning our children into a generation of super achievers, who

can do so very much that they have almost forgotten how to be."[5]

To those who might recognize a lack of lifestyle balance, hear the word of the Lord, *STOP IT!* Take stock. Evaluate your life choices. Make wise decisions that will bring life back into balance. Very few people burn-out because they have no choice. Most who do so are chasing an impossible or unrealistic dream. For some the principle of sabbath-rest might well mean "trading down," settling for cheaper, selling unnecessary liabilities, or lowering ambitions. Do whatever it takes to bring your life into balance.

2. An accent on worship

If all that is understood of the sabbath-rest principle is a greater focus on leisure and recreation, a really important point has been missed. The Sabbath is also about setting aside time to focus on God and giving him the chance to recharge our spiritual batteries.

A humorous description of a relatively new medical condition, known as *Morbus Sabbaticus*, makes the point:

> " . . . a disease peculiar to some church members. The symptoms vary, but are generally observed, and never last more than twenty-four hours. The symptoms never interfere with the appetite, nor affect the eyes. The Sunday paper can be read with no pain. The TV seems to help the eyes. No doctor is ever called. The patient begins to improve almost immediately after the church services start. No symptoms are usually felt on Saturday. The patient sleeps well and wakes feeling well. He eats a hearty Sunday breakfast, but then the attack comes and lasts until services are over for the morning. The patient then feels better and the problem seems to go away after eating a solid dinner. After dinner, he takes a nap and then watches one or two pro-football games on TV. He may go fishing or work in his yard and feels well enough to do whatever he pleases. He may take a walk before supper and stop and chat with neighbors. If there are church

5. Warner, Rob, *The Ten Commandments and the Decline of the West*, p 68.

services scheduled for Sunday evenings, he will likely have a relapse about an hour before service time. Invariably, he will wake up on Monday morning and rush off to work with no ill effects from the attack the day before. The symptoms will surely appear again the afternoon of the midweek service and probably the following Sunday as well. After a few of these "attacks" at weekly intervals, the disease seems to become chronic, it becomes worse and, for some, even terminal. Some are so affected that they quit going to church altogether . . . "[6]

In God's economy, the actual day of the week probably doesn't matter much, but the principle of having a day set aside in the context of a busy week, where God is the priority focus, is a way of keeping the fourth commandment. That was clearly the example that Jesus gave us, and it was apparently a pattern of lifestyle that he learned from his parents:

> 16 He went to Nazareth, where he had been brought up, and on the Sabbath day he went into the synagogue, as was his custom.

Luke 4:16

Now, as noted above, and in light of Jesus' own commentary on sabbath-keeping, the issue for Jesus was probably not about time and place as some have argued. Rather it is about the custom or habit of Jesus who set aside a time in the week where he gathered for corporate worship and instruction. Surely, his example should also be pretty good motivation for us! It may also lay behind the challenge given by the writer of the book of Hebrews:

> 24 And let us consider how we may spur one another on toward love and good deeds. 25 Let us not give up meeting together, as some are in the habit of doing, but let us encourage one another—and all the more as you see the Day approaching.

Hebrews 10:24–25

6. Seller, Jack, "The Pastors Desktop, Morbus Sabbaticus"

The focus or point of Sabbath worship is three-fold. Christ-followers should prioritize gathering to worship:

a. *For God's sake*—offering him our sacrifice of praise

b. *For our sake*—allowing God to minister to, teach and refresh his children

c. *For other people's sake*—that we might encourage and spur others on in their spiritual journey.

If Sunday is regarded as a Christian Sabbath, it is much more than merely a day off work. Sadly, there is an erroneous and unhealthy trend along these lines in many Christian circles. If our concept of Sabbath only means leisure or rest, our perception of the Sabbath is too small. Not only is it to be treated it as a day away from work, or a day of recreation, but also to be set aside as a *holy day*—a day that's different from the other seven; a day that focuses attention back onto God and who we are as his people, representing his purposes in our world.

The principle of Sabbath, and keeping it holy, calls to mind the thought-provoking philosophical question, "Do we see ourselves as human-beings having a spiritual experience or are we more correctly spiritual-beings having a human experience?" [7] As beings created in the image of God, we are designed with the need to worship and commune with our Creator. In gathering with God's people—making the act of worship the priority of the day, and corporate worship the priority of the week—God in turn ministers to us. He builds us up, he equips us and empowers us for the week ahead. He heals us from the bruises of the week we have just had. Sabbath-rest within the context of worship is like the recharging of our batteries.

A closing thought: While the Sabbath represented the final day of God's work-week in creation, it was also the first day of humankind's existence. We were created on Day Six, so chronologically, life for human beings actually begins with worship!

7. Huie, Jonathan Lockwood, "Pierre Teilhard de Chardin"

May the words of Isaiah be a promise taken to heart in learning to obey the fourth commandment:

> 13 "If you keep your feet from breaking the Sabbath and from doing as you please on my holy day, if you call the Sabbath a delight and the LORD's holy day honorable, and if you honor it by not going your own way and not doing as you please or speaking idle words, 14 then you will find your joy in the LORD, and I will cause you to ride on the heights of the land and to feast on the inheritance of your father Jacob." The mouth of the LORD has spoken.

Isaiah 58:13,14

Small Group Discussion Questions

1. What is your favorite recreational activity, that recharges your "batteries?"

2. What do you consider to be the right response from Christians/churches toward the liberalizing of legislation regarding retail trading on religious holidays?

3. What impact has sportsmen/women had in refusing to play sport on a Sunday—because it is the Sabbath?

4. How would you explain the meaning of Mark 2:27 to someone who was new to the Christian faith?

5. What could you do (either immediately or in the medium-term future) to bring your busy life into more balance?

6. Why do some Christians undervalue the principle of gathering together for corporate worship?

7. What will you do differently this week for considering this passage of scripture?

Chapter 5

Honorable Honor

THE GRIMM BROTHERS, JACOB & Wilhelm, lived in Germany in the first half of the nineteenth century and were renowned for publishing a series of children's stories. *Grimm's Fairy Tales* include many stories children around the world have grown up with. Early editions of their work were criticized for being labeled "children's tales" when the subject matter was not always suitable for children. One of their stories, *"The Old Man & His Grandson,"* offered a stinging commentary on how some families treat their elderly:

> "There was once a very old man, whose eyes had become dim, his ears dull of hearing, his knees trembled, and when he sat at table he could hardly hold the spoon and spilled the broth upon the table-cloth or let it run out of his mouth. His son and his son's wife were disgusted at this, so the old grandfather, at last, had to sit in the corner behind the stove, and they gave him his food in an earthenware bowl, and not even enough of it. And he used to look towards the table with his eyes full of tears.
>
> Once, his trembling hands could not hold the bowl, and it fell to the ground and broke. The young wife scolded him, but he said nothing and only sighed. Then they brought him a wooden bowl for a few half-pence, out of which he had to eat.

They were once sitting thus when the little grandson of four years old began to gather together some bits of wood upon the ground. "What are you doing there?" asked the father.

"I am making a little trough," answered the child, "for father and mother to eat out of when I am big."

The man and his wife looked at each other for a while and presently began to cry. Then they took the old grandfather to the table, and henceforth always let him eat with them, and likewise said nothing if he did spill a little of anything."[1]

The fifth of the ten values or moral guidelines that God gave the newly emerging nation of Israel was all about intergenerational respect:

12 Honor your father and your mother, so that you may live long in the land the LORD your God is giving you.

Exodus 20:12

Taken as a whole, the Ten Commandments fall naturally into two sections. In the first four commandments, the focus is clearly on our relationship with God—where he sits in our worldview and how important it is to treat him as the unrivaled focus of our life. This commandment is the first in the second section. These commandments focus more on our relationship with other people. God has given moral and relational boundaries so that there is order and peace within the community of his people.

The first of these interpersonal guidelines is about order and honor in the home. Indeed, it's been suggested that the fifth commandment is the pivotal value on which the whole ten rest. The values we learn in our homes, and especially learning to love and honor our parents, form the basis from which we learn to honor and love God, whom Jesus taught us to refer to as our Father in Heaven. The concept of loving and honoring God and respecting

---

1. Lit2Go, *Grimm Brothers—The Old Man and his Grandson*

and getting along with those with whom we share the planet, flow from these relationships and behaviors in our early years.

In fact, many social commentators, such as Pope John Paul II, have noted: "as goes the family, so goes the nation, and so goes the whole world in which we live." [2] Where there is love and order within families, there is peace and love and order in the world. Where there is chaos and dysfunction and rebellion in families, this is also reflected in society. If we think our world is becoming more debased and violent year by year, perhaps the answer lies in the foundations of life learned in the home.

While some challenge the political correctness of this kind of analysis, a 1987 study of violent rapists found that 60 percent of them came from single-parent homes. A Michigan State University study of adolescents who committed homicides found that 75 percent of them were from broken homes. Girls without fathers also become sexually active sooner and are more likely to have out-of-wedlock children.[3] Learning how to love and honor our parents is a key means of learning how to relate to our fellow men and women.

That said, the task of being a parent is not always easy. Raising children is a complex and stressful occupation. While parents love their children to bits, there are also times when children try their parents' patience and may also cause trauma, grief or anxiety. As children grow and mature they become more independent and resourceful, and at times the role of being a parent is deeply painful as children experiment with their emerging independence and individuality. It has been suggested that being a parent of teenagers is God's way of getting back at adults for enjoying sex!

Consider these two statements:

> "We are living in a dying and decadent age. Youth is corrupt, lacking in respect for its elders."[4]

2. Quotationsbook.com, Pope John Paul IIhttp://quotationsbook.com/quote/14277

3. Dobson, J. & Bauer, G; *Children at Risk*, p.167–168.

4. Flynn, Leslie B, *Now A Word from Our Creator*, p.74

"The world is passing through troublous times. The young people of today think of nothing but themselves. They have no reverence for parents or old age. They are impatient of all restraint, talk as if they know everything and what passes for wisdom with us, is foolishness with them."[5]

Lest we're tempted to think the issue of youthful rebellion against parents is a new phenomenon in our contemporary age, the first of these quotations is a translation of an inscription on an ancient Egyptian tomb. The second is a paragraph from a sermon preached by Peter the Hermit in 1274 AD. For those currently parenting individuating teenagers, it might be cold comfort to realize that the stress endured in doing so has been the plight of families all through the ages. Mark Twain is alleged to have once said, "When I was 14 years old my father was so ignorant I hated to have the old man around, but when I was 21 years old I was astonished to see how much my father had learned in only 7 years."[6]

It does, however, need to be acknowledged that there are many people who grew up in highly dysfunctional families where keeping the fifth commandment is a really big ask. Honor and respect for someone is usually earned and that isn't always possible in these homes. How parents treat their children has a huge influence on how easy their children find it to love and honor them in return. So, as well as a challenge to children about how they relate to their parents, this commandment also offers a challenge to parents to be *honor-able*.

Some of us grew up in homes where fathers and/or mothers were abusive and unkind. Maybe it was the abuse of neglect or violence. Maybe it was the abuse of overindulgence—where children learned to get whatever they wanted by throwing a tantrum. Many people carry life-long scars of discipline from parents who were out of balance on strictness. Martin Luther grew up in a family like that, where the discipline from his father was harsh and cruel. He

5. Barclay, William, *The Ten Commandments*, p.49–50.

6. Ezrachints, *Honor Thy Father and Thy Mother*

later wrote, "Spare the rod and spoil the child, true, but alongside the rod keep an apple to encourage him when he does well." [7]

Interestingly, when the Apostle Paul wrote about this particular commandment in his letter to Christians in Ephesus he added a little commentary on fair parenting:

> 1 Children, obey your parents in the LORD, for this is right. 2 "Honor your father and mother"—which is the first commandment with a promise— 3 "so that it may go well with you and that you may enjoy long life on the earth." 4 Fathers, do not exasperate your children; instead, bring them up in the training and instruction of the LORD .
>
> Ephesians 6:1–4

In other words, don't make it hard for children to honor their parents. Parents of children who give them a hard time need to not only think through strategies for fair discipline and punishment, they also may need to take a look in the mirror. Might rebellious behavior be a learned response to exasperation? Maybe some children simply haven't been given the focus, face-time, and interest that will lead them to *want* to honor their parents.

There is a *quid pro quo* element to the fifth commandment. Honor and respect may well be the yield, or return on investment, for love and fairness and deliberate energy given to our children in their developmental years. Like the comment that a son made to his father when the two of them were climbing a steep mountain, "Choose a good path Dad, I'm right behind you."

But having noted the role parents have to play, we cannot escape the fact that the fifth commandment is directed primarily at children. This is not a commandment just for those who come from good and stable families. There is no exemption clause here for those brought up in unhappy and cruel families. This is a command or a standard for all of God's people. The Bible is quite clear, those who dishonor their father and mother are actually dishonoring God.

7. Barclay, William, *New Daily Study Bible: Ephesians* (Westminster John Knox Press, 2004), Commentary on Ephesians 6:1–4

In the book of Leviticus, the Law of Moses took this issue so seriously that it gave the same harsh punishment to its repudiation as for the sin of blasphemy:

> 9 Anyone who curses their father or mother is to be put to death. Because they have cursed their father or mother, their blood will be on their own head.

Leviticus 20:9

The writer of the book of Proverbs likewise makes at least two comments on the importance of honoring parents:

> 20 If someone curses their father or mother their lamp will be snuffed out in pitch darkness.

Proverbs 20:20

> 17 The eye that mocks a father, that scorns an aged mother, will be pecked out by the ravens of the valley, will be eaten by the vultures.

Proverbs 30:17

This is a serious matter. One of the foundational institutions that God holds dear is the home. The relationship children have with their parents is extremely important in learning to relate to others, and with God himself. Therefore, God calls us to honor our parents. Whether good or bad, we are to honor our father and mother.

Perhaps the question needs to be asked, "Why does God demand this of us?" For those who come from warm and secure home backgrounds, this is an easy command to obey. For those with parents that were distant or cruel, abusive, alcoholic, or severely depressed, this is a much bigger ask. There are several positive reasons why God expects such behavior. Consider these three specific benefits that derive from honoring our fathers and mothers. The Bible teaches:

1. Our lives are blessed as a result of honoring our parents

> 12 Honor your father and your mother, so that you may live long in the land the LORD your God is giving you.
>
> Exodus 20:12

In Deuteronomy 5 there is a parallel rendition of the Ten Commandments. They are virtually identical, except that for this particular command there is an additional promise:

> 16 "Honor your father and your mother, as the LORD your God has commanded you, so that you may live long and that it may go well with you in the land the LORD your God is giving you.
>
> Deuteronomy 5:16

Those who honor their father and mother will prosper. Life will go well for them. The blessing and peace of God will be their experience. Perhaps one of the ways this might be encountered is through receiving the same honor and respect from their own children when they are old and infirm. Children learn how to care for and honor their parents, by watching the way their mothers and fathers care for their grandparents.

Growing old is a scary experience; it's not for the faint-hearted! We started out in life totally dependent on others, and then moved to independence and self-sufficiency. As the years advance, however, the independence pendulum swings back in the opposite direction. We can often become dependent again on others for our care, transport, and welfare. The prospect of losing our independence is a deeply frightening thought. "Who will be there for me?" Those who modeled honor and respect for their parents in the past will most likely have provided a template for how their own children might care for them when their turn comes around. They may face the future with a greater sense of peace and confidence; what goes around is likely to come around!

2. Honoring parents is the right thing to do

When Paul wrote on this theme he appealed to moral judgment:

> 1Children, obey your parents in the LORD, for this is right . . .
>
> Ephesians 6:1

There are some things God asks of us irrespective of whether we understand the reason why. It is just the right thing to do. So much of contemporary culture guides behavior with fickle feelings and emotions. Determination of right from wrong behavior can be more driven by mood or popular opinion than objective values that are set for us by God. Sometimes doing the right thing by God is not what people might choose to do because they are intellectually convinced or emotionally motivated.

Maybe for those who come from very dysfunctional families, honoring one's father and mother is one of those occasions where "special grace is required." It has to come as grace-imparted from God in order for these individuals to be able to achieve it. It may not be what some feel like doing. It may not even be natural justice in light of how they've been treated, but it is still the right thing to do. In honoring one's parents we comply with God's standards, and doesn't he have a pretty impressive track record of loving those who don't deserve it!

3. Honoring parents pleases God

The New Testament letter to the Colossians is very similar in its themes to the letter to the Ephesians. When Paul talked about family relationships with the Colossians he put it like this:

> 20 Children, obey your parents in everything, for this pleases the LORD.
>
> Colossians 3:20

God is pleased with those who obey his counsel. Given who God is, and all that he does, and all that he is capable of doing, surely it is far better to earn God's pleasure than his displeasure. To dishonor one's parents is to dishonor God. To obey God's command, and treat one's parents well, is the kind of behavior that earns God's reward. God is close and reveals himself to those who obey his instructions. It was Jesus who said:

> 21 Whoever has my commands and keeps them is the one who loves me. The one who loves me will be loved by my Father, and I too will love them and show myself to them."

John 14:21

Well, enough of the injunctions; how is this to be done? What does the concept of honoring parents actually look like? In terms of definitions, the word "honor" means literally to esteem highly or regard as being of great value. We honor a person by recognizing them as having influence, dignity, and authority. We defer to them as people of importance. There are obviously myriads of opportunities for the expression of honor toward parents. Here are four specific suggestions:

1. Gratitude

We honor our parents by thanking them for the care and nurture they have demonstrated towards us. We owe our very being to our parents. Sure, there were times when they made us really mad, and we believed we had the cruelest and most old-fashioned parents in the world. But think of all the times they were there when as children we were sick or when we'd fallen and skinned our knees. We exist today because a parent cradled us as a baby and fed us and clothed us in our growing years.

There's a delightful story of a mother who had skimped and saved to put her son through his tertiary education. She sat with great pride among the audience on the day he graduated, and she watched as her son walked across the platform and received his degree with honors. As he walked down the aisle, instead of turning into the designated row for graduating students, he kept walking. People watched as he broke ranks with all the other students and walked up into the audience, right up to where his mother was sitting. The young man threw his arms around her neck, kissed her on the cheek, and as he placed his diploma in her hands said, "Here mother, you have earned this!" [8]

There are times when other people may not have believed in us and wanted to write us off. Our mother probably wasn't one of them. Maybe it's not too late to honor our parents (either in person or in speaking of their memory) by giving thanks for the love and care they lavished upon us in our growing years?

2. Listening to their advice

Parents are honored when we allow them to speak into our lives. In many respects, their technological knowledge may not be as advanced as that of their children, since so much communication technology and scientific knowledge has been developed in recent decades. However, our parents have years' more experience on their "life-clock" than their children. That's not to say that their advice will be infallible, but it is always worth listening to.

There's a Christian principle here worth grasping. 1 Peter 5:5 says:

> 5 . . . you who are younger, submit yourselves to your elders

Those who have lived longer have experience to offer those who are young, and those who are young honor those who are older by listening attentively to their experiences. Or as the writer of Proverbs put it:

> 15 The way of fools seems right to him, but the wise listen to advice.
>
> Proverbs 12:15

8. Trivette, Ken, *Sermonsearch*.

3. Supporting them in their old age

There is a wise saying, "Be kind to your children for they will choose your retirement home!"

The Bible explicitly teaches us the necessity of honoring our parents in their old age by caring for their welfare and attending to their physical, social and emotional needs. Paul wrote to Timothy about this in 1 Timothy 5. In the early days of the Christian church, there was a special "poor fund" that provided material care for widows and orphans. In the absence of a welfare state, such people were otherwise forced to beg for survival, and the early church exercised a special ministry toward them. Indeed, the Roman church by the middle of the third century had as many as 1500 needy persons whom they supported.[9] Apparently though, even in its early years, the system was open to abuse. Some widows were placed on the official list of recipients even though they had family nearby who were quite capable of caring for their needs. The problem had reached a point that Paul needed to clarify the eligibility criteria for the fund:

> 3 Give proper recognition to those widows who are really in need. 4 But if a widow has children or grandchildren, these should learn first of all to put their religion into practice by caring for their own family and so repaying their parents and grandparents, for this is pleasing to God.

1 Timothy 5:3,4

This might be one of those verses we ask our friends to send to our respective children! The biblical injunction is quite clear, if aging parents are in need, the first responsibility for their care rests with their family. We honor our parents by looking after their needs as they age and can no longer take care of themselves.

These days, in many parts of the world, people tend to look to the government to do this kind of work. Grizzles can be heard when the government won't pay for the care of aged parents until or unless all their assets have been exhausted. Better that aged

9. Hengel, Martin. *"Property and Riches in the Early Church,"* (p. 42–44

parents' estates are kept intact or ring-fenced so that their children can inherit! Surely there is not much difference between these contemporary attitudes and practices, and those families in the early church who put widows on the church's "poor list" when their extended family had the means to look after them. Such behavior is morally wrong. We honor our parents by caring for them when they lose their independence. Even if it means a measure of inconvenience, it is the right thing to do.

4. Forgive them

Every child has at least some memory of pain and sadness associated with their parents. It's inevitable—our parents are/were human, and at times they failed.

As noted, for some people the painful memories outweigh the happy ones. The saddest and most difficult funeral I have ever taken was for the father of an only child whom he had sexually abused over several years. Some people said they came to the funeral to make sure the b*****d was really dead!

Maybe parents were not good at their task and the growing up years were full of pain. Perhaps our parents are still alive, maybe they have passed away; followers of Jesus live in a new and different paradigm to the rest of the world. They live in the glow of God's love and grace and mercy. God has renewed them, restored them, and is in the process of rebuilding them. Part of that renewal process may well be learning to forgive those who have caused us hurt and pain in the past. The counsel of the Scriptures is clear, and if such people were our parents, Christ followers also learn how to forgive them for their past mistakes. To retain hostility in our hearts toward a father or mother is to limit one's own experience of God's grace and love. Maybe one-way such parents can be honored is by forgiving them, and where possible attempting to restore that damaged relationship.

This chapter closes with a quote from a controversial comedian. Bill Cosby has been in the news in recent years for all the wrong reasons, but he once made an interesting comment about the very first parent:

> Whenever your kids are out of control you can take comfort from the thought that even God's omnipotence did not extend to his children. After creating Heaven and Earth, God created Adam and Eve and the first thing God said to them was "Don't!"
>
> "Don't what?" Adam asked.
>
> "Don't eat the forbidden fruit," said God.
>
> "Forbidden fruit? Really? Where is it?" Adam and Eve asked jumping up and down excitedly.
>
> "It's over there," said God, wondering why he hadn't stopped after making the elephant. A few minutes later God saw the kids having an apple break and he was very angry: "Didn't I tell you not to eat that fruit?" the first parent asked.
>
> "Ah huh."
>
> "Then why did you do it?" God asked exasperatedly.
>
> "I dunno," Adam answered.
>
> The first parent's punishment was that Adam and Eve should have children of their own! [10]

---

10. Cosby, Bill; *Fatherhood*, p. 65.

Small Group Discussion Questions

1. What is the warmest memory you have of your mother or father?

2. Why do values learned in the home have such an impact on how we relate with others in adult life?

3. Is there ever a case or justification for dishonoring our parents?

4. What is the hardest aspect of being a parent? How did you make parenting difficult for your mother and father?

5. What do you consider to be a Christian response to nursing homes and retirement villages for elderly people?

6. How would apply the principle Paul made in 1 Timothy 5:3–4

7. What could you do this week to honor your father and mother?

Chapter 6

Killer Instincts

OVER A PERIOD OF weeks, a Sunday School teacher was teaching a class of eight-year-old children about the Ten Commandments. One Sunday, as they reviewed the lesson from the previous week about honoring our father and mother, she innocently asked the question, "Can anyone think of a commandment in the Bible regarding brothers and sisters?"

After a moment's silence, one young girl waved her hand very excitedly with the response, "Thou shalt not kill!"

That's the next value or moral boundary in the Ten Commandments that God set out for the emerging Jewish nation—camped in a desert, *en route* to their promised land. Four short words:

13 You shall not murder . . .

Exodus 20:13

Now, some might wonder what there is to discuss about this particular commandment? Isn't it obvious; just *don't!*

In point of fact, this particular verse has been the source of considerable debate and dispute over the years, particularly in terms of its reach and implications. Does this commandment apply to all forms of killing, or is it more specifically focused on the crime of murder? For instance, have Buddhists, vegetarians and vegans got it right in arguing that animals not be killed for food, or does it apply to just human beings? Older English translations use the word "killing," whereas some of the newer translations (like the NIV) say the original Hebrew word meant specifically the act of murder—as in the violent and unauthorized killing of someone. [1]

Thinking it through further, several questions begin to surface: Is this a commandment that prohibits any cessation of human life beyond the usual processes of aging, sickness or accident? Does it apply to killing in the form of abortion, euthanasia or suicide? Does it apply to capital punishment or acts of war that also kill people? Does it imply that Christians ought not to serve in the armed forces, because that is an industry that specifically trains its members in how to kill an enemy? Are there some forms of killing that can be sanctioned or justified—maybe as recompense for something evil or heinous that a person has done? Is the dropping of a nuclear bomb unjustifiable even when responding to another nation doing the same? If "You shall not murder" applies to all forms of killing, does this commandment allow for punishing someone for an accidental death—like road deaths or manslaughter? What about the person who kills in self-defense or while defending their family and property?

These are all complex ethical and theological issues about which we may have differing opinions. For many of the arguments around issues like the "sanctity of life," there are many other passages of Scripture that can be drawn upon to clarify or apply the four words in this sixth commandment.[2] Suffice it to say, the definition of murder in this commandment specifically refers to the *"unlawful killing of a human being with malice aforethought."*[3] It is premeditated murder; the ending of someone's life as a result of hatred or selfish intent.

Most people at this point could probably score a positive "check" alongside this commandment. Some of the other

1. William Barclay, *"The Ten Commandments,"* p.52.

2. See God's advice to Noah after the flood in Genesis 9:5–6

3. *The Random House College Dictionary,* p.877

commandments might give cause for pause, but not this one. "We have got this one right! I have never taken the life of another person out of hate or malice . . . what else is there to say . . . move on to the next commandment."

However, it might be possible that Jesus would want to say, "Hang on a minute . . . not so fast!" Reading this commandment through the interpretive lens of Jesus might suggest some additional issues about killing that are worthy of consideration.

Indeed, that's exactly what he did for the people of his generation—around 1500 years after this commandment was given. In Matthew's biography on the life of Jesus, he records a well-known sermon that Jesus gave in the early years of his ministry. The basic content of Jesus' discourse was a clarification of the intent or heart of many ancient laws that God gave to the Jews during the time of Moses, because of the way they were being misconstrued in his day. Since the time of Moses, and especially in the few hundred years prior to the time of Jesus, religious teachers had done horrible things to the Mosaic Law, reducing it to a long list of specific and often pedantic legal definitions. In many instances, this resulted in the spirit behind them being missed, forgotten or deliberately overlooked. In his sermon, Jesus reiterated the original meaning or divine intent of these laws. He commented specifically on this commandment about murder:

> 21 "You have heard that it was said to the people long ago, 'You shall not murder, and anyone who murders will be subject to judgment.' 22 But I tell you that anyone who is angry with a brother or sister will be subject to judgment. Again, anyone who says to a brother or sister, 'Raca,' is answerable to the court. And anyone who says, 'You fool!' will be in danger of the fire of hell.

> 23 "Therefore, if you are offering your gift at the altar and there remember that your brother or sister has something against you, 24 leave your gift there in front of the altar. First go and be reconciled to them; then come and offer your gift.

> Matthew 5:21–24

Looking through the lens of Jesus, there is a bit more to this issue of murder than what we might initially perceive. According to Jesus, murder begins in the heart, not in the hands. It's the flip side to the saying that many of us grew up with, "It's the thought that counts!"

As a humorous aside, Ruth Graham, the wife of the late evangelist Billy Graham, was interviewed about her marriage. She recounted a conversation she had with a reporter who had suggested that it couldn't have been easy having a husband like hers, who traveled extensively and was constantly in the public spotlight. The reporter apparently asked whether she had ever entertained the thought of being married to someone else; had she ever contemplated divorce? Her response was swift: "No, I've never thought of divorce in all these 35 years of marriage, but," she said, "I did think of murder a few times . . ." [4]

Jesus' commentary in the Sermon the Mount makes clear, the concept of murder is not merely the extinguishing of life and breath from a person. Murder or the destruction of another person's life begins with an attitude of the heart. By that definition, a lot more people might be feeling guilty than there were at the outset of this chapter? Jesus suggested at least three ways that we might unwittingly be guilty of breaking the sixth commandment:

1. Through anger towards another person

22 But I tell you that anyone who is angry with a brother
or sister will be subject to judgment . . .

What did Jesus mean here? On the surface, this sounds rather harsh! The King James Version adds the words "without cause," perhaps trying to soften it a little, but the earliest Greek manuscripts don't support that additional qualification.

If anger is synonymous with murder in the eyes of God, no doubt all people are guilty. Who at some time has not become

---

4. Gibbs, Nancy and Duffy, Michael, *Time: Ruth Graham, Soulmate to Billy, Dies,*l

angry at someone over something said or done? There might even be a case for claiming Jesus himself was guilty of murder; didn't he become angry at the money-changers and merchants in the temple when he made a whip and drove them out? [5]

When we investigate the original language in which his words are recorded, there's a specific type of anger that Jesus is referring to here. The Greek language of the New Testament contains two words that have been translated into English as *anger*. The first is the word *thumos*; describing an anger that flares up, and then calms down just as quickly.[6] Picture the flame that comes from dried straw or hay that is set alight; this type of anger flares up quickly and blazes with ferocity, like a hay barn on fire, but then dies down just as quickly when all the fuel is consumed. It doesn't last or linger.

The second word is *orgê*,[7] referring to the kind of anger that is long-lived and continuous. It describes the anger of someone who nurses their wrath in order to keep it warm; anger that broods, and nurses bitterness and resentment—sometimes for years or generations.

This second type of anger is what Jesus referred to when he equated it with the sin of murder. Everyone becomes angry and loses their cool at some point, and while this might not be warranted or productive, it is also relatively normal. The kind of anger that Jesus was talking about was more serious than that. Not so much hot-headed emotion, but rather cool and calculating. Revenge is a dish best served cold! An anger that broods and stews and refuses to forget—perhaps even wishing the other party removed from the situation or even dead.

Jesus quite clearly states that such anger toward another person is nothing short of murder in the eyes of God. We may not have actually shot the person with a gun, but the intent to do so, or to think of doing so, is tantamount to the same thing.

5. Cf. Matthew 21:12–13; Mark 11:15–18; John 2:13–17

6. William Barclay, *The Daily Study Bible–The Gospel of Matthew Vol. 1*, p.138.

7. Ibid, p.138

In this sense, the sixth commandment raises challenging questions: Are there people towards whom we nurture a grudge, or against whom we allow our anger to keep simmering? A next-door neighbor once revealed that she hadn't spoken to her brother for forty years because of a silly argument they'd had. She spoke of him with venom, and her eyes and body language expressed her anger and hatred.

The law of our land may well say that a person is guilty of homicide only when they deliberately cause another's death, but Jesus said that in God's view murder is more pervasive. Anger in the heart of a man or woman that wishes their adversary were dead or hopes for some other kind of calamitous outcome in vengeance, is just the same as actually killing them.

2. Through contempt and discrimination

> Again, anyone who says to a brother or sister, 'Raca,' is answerable to the court . . .

Jesus' point here requires a bit of explanation. The word *raca* is almost impossible to translate into English, which is why a number of translations have simply imported the original word into the text. It referred more to the tone of voice used than to any actual description of a person. It was like an overtone of contempt that a person felt toward someone else.[8] To call someone "*raca!*" was an act of deep insult. It was a colossal put-down; regarding the recipient as inherently inferior, useless or depraved.

Essentially it is the sin of discrimination, where a person regards him or herself as a cut above another. Racial discrimination or ethnic stereotyping would be an example; regarding the color of skin as an indication of intellectual and moral inferiority. Socio-economic discrimination or snobbery might be another example, where people of wealth are regarded as inherently superior, more sophisticated and intelligent than those who are at the poorer end of the demographic.

8. Ibid, p.139

When Jesus said these words, he wasn't referring only to name calling. It was more serious than that. It was the attitude of contempt and discrimination that accompanied it, in effect regarding another person as a no-hoper, useless or "trash." The effect was to destroy the person's hope of change or improvement; murdering their dream of bettering themselves. In the context of home or school today, it might be recognized in the repeated labeling of a child as "dumb," "thick," or "clumsy," or comparing them unfavorably to an older sibling: "Why can't you be like . . . ?" Such verbal information is received by the spirit of a person and can become the blueprint for their development. It manifests itself *information*. It restricts opportunity and puts the recipient at risk of becoming that which they were called.

Jesus said that such contempt and discrimination held by one person towards another is nothing less than the crime of murder. Put simply, all forms of racism and racial profiling are evil and antithetical to a Christian worldview! Only God has the right to discriminate over a person's character and worth—and if the Bible is anything to go by, he chooses not to do so. Through discrimination and prejudice, we destroy the future potential of another person created in the image of God. God regards such discrimination as seriously as if we took that person's life.

3. Through Character Assassination

> And anyone who says, 'You fool!' will be in danger of the fire of hell.

Once again, Jesus' words require some contextual understanding. The real impact of Jesus' prohibition had to do with the meaning of the original word he chose. The word translated as *"fool"* was the word *moros* (from which we get a word like *moron* that has been used in a derogatory way towards someone who seems slow or mentally impaired). In its original Greek context, however, it didn't refer so much to intellectual foolishness (as in a low I.Q. or being intellectually slower), as to moral foolishness. It was more serious by way of an insult. It described the person who "plays the fool" or who "fools around" in terms of moral conduct.[9]

Jesus wasn't talking about insulting a person by calling them intellectually dull or stupid, he was referring to the more serious crime of labeling a person as immoral or depraved. He was talking about creating a slur on the moral character of another person. The sin of gossiping about another behind his or her back or spreading vicious and malicious rumors that destroy a person's reputation in their community, is regarded as seriously as the crime of ending someone's life.

To give a frightening modern-day example, it could be likened to the damage done to a person wrongly accused of sexual abuse. Regardless of proof and evidence, mud sticks. A man can lose his job, his family and his friends because someone starts a rumor that he sexually abuses children. To cite a personal example, many years ago as a young pastor I took a Social Welfare worker to meet the family of a little boy who had come into the orbit of our church. He had clearly been sexually abused, but no one at that stage knew by whom. His sexualized play at school was deeply disruptive and disturbing. As we got back into my car after meeting with the family the Social Worker nonchalantly said to me: "It's definitely the father! I can see it in his eyes!" Later on, when the truth finally came out, it wasn't the father at all, but an uncle who had been showing his nephew pornographic videos. However, the damage had already been done to the father's reputation.

That is the kind of vicious character assassination that Jesus is talking about. Words carelessly spoken can be like deadly poison, and the Bible counsels us to keep a tight rein on our tongues. Some might think they would never assassinate the character of another person—we're not guilty of that! But consider whether when we listen to or allow someone to tell us a juicy piece of gossip about another person, or when we pass on what we have heard to someone else, we become an accomplice to the crime.

9. William Barclay, *The Daily Study Bible–The Gospel of Matthew Vol. 1*, p.140.

Murder, according to Jesus' definition, was not merely the intentional ending of another person's life. In some respects, that might have been the kinder thing. It is often far more painful and hurtful to be the object of another person's hate-filled anger, discrimination or character assassination. The act of murder does not begin in the hands of the murderer, but in his or her heart.

But then Jesus went a step further! He went on to associate the hate-filled attitude of a person's heart toward other people, with their fruitless attempts at having a right relationship with God. To the people of Jesus' day, righteousness and acceptability before God was achieved by doing all the correct acts of worship or outward displays of religion and ritual. Jesus maintained that it was hugely different to that. Outward acts of worship and religious ceremony are rendered absolutely useless, and even abhorrent to God unless they represent an inward attitude of the heart that is genuine:

> 23 "Therefore, if you are offering your gift at the altar and there remember that your brother or sister has something against you, 24 leave your gift there in front of the altar. First go and be reconciled to them; then come and offer your gift.

> Matthew 5:23–24

The idea behind the Jewish sacrifice was simple. If a person did something wrong and committed a sin, that action was said to disturb or inhibit relationship with God. The Bible defines God as holy, and therefore unable to have anything to do with that which is sinful. Sin, therefore, causes the rift or a separation between man and God. Jewish sacrifice was a God-given means of restoring this broken relationship with God—perhaps in a similar way that we might pay a fine for a traffic or driving offense today. As a symbolic act of their repentance, the person would sacrifice or give up an animal (or a bird or a crop) as a substitutionary restitution for their sin. The sacrifice on the altar became a substitute for the person who had done wrong and deserved to be punished.[10] Justice

---

10. Leviticus 17:11

was said to have been satisfied, and the penitent sinner declared to be in a right relationship with God once more.

For the Jews of Jesus' day, the sacrificial system had become rather sterile and mechanical. Almost as if: "It doesn't matter what we do, or what the attitude of our heart is like, so long as we offer the sacrifice everything will be okay!" Jesus, like the Old Testament prophets who preceded him, suggested the attitude of the heart is actually more important than the actual sacrifice.

Jesus also applied that principle to our relationships with other people. Restoration of friendship with God (being made righteous) cannot be complete until there has been a corresponding setting right of our broken relationships with others. To be more graphic, I cannot punch you in the nose and then go and expect God to accept my sacrifice of praise and worship. First, I must come back to you and seek your forgiveness and put our relationship to right, then my worship of God is likely to be acceptable.

One of the more dominant themes throughout the New Testament is that true and genuine relationship with God requires of us a right relationship with other people. The two go hand in hand. It is not possible to have a *snitch* against another person and expect to have a close relationship with Jesus.

> 9 Anyone who claims to be in the light but hates a brother or sister is still in the darkness . . . . 11 But anyone who hates a brother or sister is in the darkness and walks around in the darkness. They do not know where they are going, because the darkness has blinded them.

> 1 John 2:9,11

> 20 Whoever claims to love God yet hates a brother or sister is a liar. For whoever does not love their brother and sister, whom they have seen, cannot love God, whom they have not seen.

> 1 John 4:20

Jesus went further than just talking about the people that *we* have a *snitch* against. He also talks about those we know who have something against *us*—even if the grudge is not reciprocated. If a person recalls that another is hurting because of something they believe we have done against them, it is incumbent upon us to try and restore that relationship. It doesn't really matter who started the rift, or who was right and who was wrong in the earlier dispute. The point is, a relationship has broken down, and until such time as that is restored (to the best of one's ability) worship before God is inhibited.

As we have seen, the sixth commandment has a bit more to it than forbidding the ending of a person's life. To know harmony with God, Jesus said, requires dealing with discord and broken relationships. In one sense that is a very humbling thing to have to do—going to someone and asking forgiveness for broken fellowship. But in another sense, it is one of the most liberating experiences a follower of Jesus can have. There is nothing quite like the sense of relief and joy at having a broken friendship restored. More than that, it brings a fresh sense of release and fellowship with God that broken friendship with others keeps at a distance.

From time to time you hear people say of broken relationships: "time will heal." In other words, there is no need to go and see the person you have offended (or who has offended you). Just leave it alone and in time it will heal. No doubt there are some situations where that might work, but in most cases, it does not. Time seldom heals. Ignoring broken relationships is a bit like putting a Band-Aid on a cancerous tumor. Covering it up so it can't be seen doesn't make it go away. A tumor needs to be cut out. Then, after the surgery, time will heal. Tumors can go into remission, to all appearances they are no longer there, but frequently they can flare into life again. The time to set a broken relationship to right is sooner, not later. The longer it is left the more painful it may be.

So, this sixth commandment has a bit more bite than first appears. On face value, a person may be tempted to think this has no relevance for them. They haven't ended someone's life with malice aforethought. However, Jesus demonstrates the issue lies a little deeper.

- How do we regard and treat others?

- What is our heart attitude toward those who are different to us?

- What have we been saying about others that might influence their reputation in the eyes of a third party?

How these kinds of questions are answered has a significant bearing on the quality of our relationship with our Father in Heaven.

Small Group Discussion Questions

1. What do you regard as the differences between murder and other forms of taking a life?

2. What kinds of situations in life make you lose your cool?

3. Jesus statement about anger (Matthew 5:22) is rather strong. How do you go about resolving a serious conflict with people?

4. What would you say is at the root cause of discrimination (e.g. racial or class) between people?

5. How have you experienced been discriminated against?

6. What are some examples you can tell (either personal or other people) of character assassination?

7. What are some contemporary ways of applying Matthew 5:23–24?

8. What will you do differently this week for considering this seventh commandment?

Chapter 7

God and Sex: How Do They Mix?

(If your first perusal of this book was via the Table of Contents, it's possible this is the first chapter turned to . . . just saying . . .)

THE STORY IS TOLD of a pastor who preached a daring sermon on the subject of sex but he chose to do so when his wife was out of town, visiting her elderly mother. When his wife got home she asked her husband what he had preached on that Sunday. He was a little embarrassed to tell her the topic of his sermon, so he told her he spoke about water-skiing. His wife thought this was a little unusual but let it ride. A couple of days later she ran into a lady from the church in the local supermarket, who remarked on how her husband was a brave man to speak so boldly on such a subject. "I never knew he was so knowledgeable about that sort of thing." To which his wife replied, "Yes, I'm a little surprised myself, he's only done it twice and both times he fell off and sprained his back."

In this chapter, we're talking about *water-skiing. . . .*!

The seventh value or behavior boundary that God gave the emerging nation of Israel is possibly a topic that is not talked about enough in church these days:

14 You shall not commit adultery

Exodus 20:14

Put bluntly, the people of God, who live their lives according to his values, have been provided with clearly defined boundaries when it comes to sexuality. The subject of sex is something about which the Bible has a lot to say, and contrary to popular opinion the perspective of the Bible is not primarily: *"Thou shalt not!"*

The definition of adultery, of course, is quite specific. It refers to sexual relations between two people—a man and a woman— who are not married to each other. One or the other is married to someone else,[1] and the act of sexual connection between them, according to the counsel of Scripture, has the effect of deeply damaging, in some cases irreparably, the marriage relationship.

When you read the Old Testament laws of Moses, adultery was not treated as a minor indiscretion. It was a serious sin that carried the death penalty, although commentators suggest that in most cases it led to divorce rather than the capital punishment being carried out.[2]

Whichever way you look at it, adultery is something God commands his people to deliberately abstain from. "Do not do it!" However, while the Bible teaches with clarity about the sin of sleeping with someone other than your husband or wife, many people over the years have mistakenly formed the view that God takes a dim view of sex and sexuality per se. The impression given is that it is a practice technically permitted, but largely frowned upon; and that spiritual people ought to avoid it if possible, as if it's something dirty and shameful. That is not actually the case. God and the Bible are decidedly pro-sex!

So, in discussing this seventh commandment perhaps the place to begin is broadening the topic from merely *"thou shalt not"* to include what it is that *"thou art free to do."* In understanding what is prohibited, one must also consider that which is allowed, and even encouraged.

1. *The Random House College Dictionary*, p.19
2. William Barclay, *The Ten Commandments*, p.86.

To be sure, the contemporary age is highly sexualized. Besotted with sex is probably not an exaggeration. Turn on the TV any night of the week, go to the movies, pick up a magazine in the doctor or dentist's waiting room, or listen to the conversation in the work lunchroom or school playground—sex is probably the most talked about, written about, analyzed, philosophized, fanaticized, and romanticized subject in the Western world. It is no longer under the covers or behind closed bedroom doors. There are no covers anymore, and the door is wide open! Everywhere one goes we are confronted with the allure or innuendo of sex. We are told how it ought to be approached, enjoyed and its experience improved.

There was a time when couples who engaged in sex before they were married kept it quiet lest they be found out. Nowadays those who don't have pre-marital sex keep their mouth shut lest they become the subject of ridicule and derision. There was a time when the burning issue for a young lady was whether or not to allow her boyfriend to kiss her on their first date. Nowadays the issue is whether she should allow him to take her to bed. There was a day when a single young man would prepare to meet his date with a bunch of flowers. Today his preparation doesn't include a trip to the florist, but rather to the pharmacy or supermarket for condoms—he may get lucky tonight! Even within the Christian book trade, countless titles on sexual fulfillment are available. Everywhere we are confronted by the issue of sexuality.

So, if sex is no longer under the covers, and if homosexuality is no longer in the closet, maybe it's time the church came out from under its religious "bushel" and found its voice on this subject. It is a topic which the church needs to openly discuss.

Despite the popular perception, the first point worth noting is that sex was God's idea! The seventh commandment was not intended to be a recommendation of abstinence. Indeed, according to the Bible, sexual intercourse and sexual intimacy are something God designed. It is part and parcel of the way God created the human race. It is not unseemly or something to be ashamed of. Sex is an integral part of God's creation, and the Bible says that when God "created" he stood back and said: "It is good." Or as one commentator expressed it: "When God created the first human being he formed him from the dust of the ground. When God created the second human being he brought her from the first one's rib. But I like the third way best!"

In other words, the act and pleasure of sex is not something that humanity devolved to because of our fall into sin. God fashioned a man in one way with sexual organs and urges. He created a woman slightly differently (some have argued as a more refined and improved model!), also with sexual organs and urges. Together men and women were created to complete and complement each other, satisfying the sexual desires which God designed and approved. Sex was God's idea!

However, God also prescribed where the fulfillment of sexual pleasure is to be experienced and this is within the confines of a marriage relationship.

To use a medical analogy, we've all visited a doctor when unwell, and received a prescription for a course of medication that will help us recover. When a person uplifts their medication from the pharmacist, there are typically important instructions on the label. Maybe something like, "Take two times a day after meals." The prescribed medication contains chemicals that will cure an ailment, but it may also contain properties that cause pain and serious discomfort to the lining of a person's stomach if taken without food.

There's a parallel here with the idea of human sexuality. God has prescribed it as something good or wholesome and fulfilling for us, however, there is a warning on the bottle, "Take as often as you like to enjoy intimacy—after marriage!" Taking it beforehand runs the risk of pain and discomfort.[3]

To restate the case: sex was God's idea! He made it possible. However, it was designed for the pleasure and fulfillment of a man and woman who have made a life-long commitment to each other in the covenant of marriage. Sexual relations outside of this condition conflicts with God's design. It doesn't fulfill, it doesn't complete, and it doesn't carry the *money-back-guarantee* of

3. Check out Solomon's advice in Proverbs 6:20–7:27!

satisfaction that sex within a marriage relationship enjoys. Despite the impression our depraved culture might promote, sex outside of marriage is a deviation from God's stated purpose and is therefore sin. Maybe it could be likened to "pill-popping" or taking someone else's medication. It may give a temporary high but the long-term effects are often disastrous.

It may not be a popular thing to say these days, but sex outside the covenant of marriage is a perversion or distortion of God's intention for the human race. Sex, which was designed to be wholesome and pleasurable has been perverted and corrupted. And the Bible makes it clear, in both the Old and the New Testaments, that deliberate and persistent refusal to live according to God's values ultimately leads to exclusion from his kingdom. The apostle Paul gave a rather severe reminder along these lines when writing to a church he knew well. Corinth was a city renowned for its sexual perversion and depravity and Paul wrote:

> 9 Do you not know that the wicked will not inherit the kingdom of God? Do not be deceived: Neither the sexually immoral nor idolaters nor adulterers nor male prostitutes nor homosexual offenders 10 nor thieves nor the greedy nor drunkards nor slanderers nor swindlers will inherit the kingdom of God. 11 And that is what some of you were.
>
> 1 Corinthians 6:9–11

Maybe it's worth noting here that slanderers and swindlers face the same fate as unrepentant sexual offenders! It is important though, that one doesn't throw out the baby with the bath water. Or along the lines of our medication analogy, just because some people take other people's medication and come to harm, doesn't mean that those same pills taken by the right people in the right way won't be good and helpful.

All of this begs an important question, if the Bible so clearly condemns the misappropriation of human sexuality (in the form of sexual relations outside of wedlock, or with those with whom we are not covenanted together in marriage), what is the right and proper expression of sexuality? What is the purpose or function of sex that God had in mind?

Many in our contemporary world have the mistaken perception that Christianity is a morally uptight religion, woefully outdated and bound by rules and regulations that prohibit pleasure and intimacy. Christianity is perceived as synonymous with loss of freedom. The opposite is actually true. Imagine what it would be like living in a society where there were no road rules or laws curbing violence or laws on the theft of property? God's values do not inhibit our freedom rather they create the space in which it can flourish.

It is worth acknowledging that over the years there have been those who believed and taught, that God created sex solely for procreation. The conception of a baby is the only reason for having sex with your partner; anything beyond that is carnal or sinful. (Indeed, many women have been harmed by bearing multiple children, often very close together because they are told that they should not deny their husbands nor take birth control. Abstinence from sex or feelings of guilt from "indulgence" is undoubtedly detrimental to a healthy marriage relationship.)

Sadly, this kind of perception is not at all consistent with what the Bible teaches. While one of the results of sexual relations is the conception of children, this is not the primary purpose of sex. God designed sexual intercourse to be the physical expression or symbol of unity or oneness between a husband and wife. Take for instance the first allusion to sex in the creation story. Genesis 2:24 says:

> 24For this reason, a man will leave his father and mother and be united to his wife, and they will become one flesh . . .

It is a physical act of becoming one flesh—joining with one's marriage partner.

When God created the human race, it was for a purpose vastly different from the rest of the animal kingdom. Human beings are created after the likeness or image of God, with the need for companionship and intimacy. Sexual desire is not something that comes upon people at certain times or seasons in the cycle of a year, as it does for animals. Enduring sexual desire and relations in a marriage are the normal physical expression of the emotional and spiritual commitment of being one unit.

There are two by-products of that physical expression of oneness. As noted, one is the "pitter-patter" of little feet. The other is pleasure. Sex between a man and a woman is not like sex between animals, neither should it be a mechanical act. It is intended to be a pleasurable experience of deep-soul communication; an act of love and tenderness, exposing the most vulnerable parts of our body to the one person we love the most and share our life with. A healthy and fulfilling sex life is commended in the Bible for married couples.

Then there are those who have been taught that sexual restraint within a marriage is somehow more holy and spiritual than frequent sexual expression. The idea being, that a person cannot maintain a close relationship with God and also be having frequent sex with their husband or wife—the two simply don't mix. The Apostle Paul would take issue with that line of reasoning. In fact, he gave some quite racy advice along these lines to the Corinthian Christians:

> 2 But since sexual immorality is occurring, each man should have sexual relations with his own wife, and each woman with her own husband. 3 The husband should fulfil his marital duty to his wife, and likewise the wife to her husband. 4 The wife does not have authority over her own body but yields it to her husband. In the same way, the husband does not have authority over his own body but yields it to his wife. 5 Do not deprive each other except perhaps by mutual consent and for a time, so that you may devote yourselves to prayer. Then come together again so that Satan will not tempt you because of your lack of self-control.
>
> 1 Corinthians 7:2–5

The wife's body, Paul says, is not her own; she must share herself with her husband. Likewise, the husband's body is not his own; he must share himself with his wife.

Josh McDowell, in his book: *"Givers Takers & Other Kinds of Lovers"* suggests: "A good sex life very seldom produces a good relationship. But a good marriage produces a fantastic sex life."[4] Perhaps that might raise the question: How often is healthy and how often isn't? Obviously, that will differ from couple to couple and for different ages and stages in life. Maybe the following humorous piece of advice is worth considering,

- Those under 45—tri-weekly.
- Those aged between 45 and 70—try weekly.
- Those over the age of 70—try weakly!

Once again, in considering the seventh commandment, which forbids sex with anyone who is not our marriage partner, we would be remiss not to look at it in the light of Jesus and his ministry. For once again, in the Sermon on the Mount, Jesus offered some important commentary. There were people in Jesus' day, as probably there also are today, who were self-righteous and smug around this prohibition. "Nope . . . never done that; never committed adultery!" Jesus again cautioned, "Hang on a minute, not quite so fast," and proceeded to give a more rigorous definition of adultery:

> 27 "You have heard that it was said, 'You shall not commit adultery.' 28 But I tell you that anyone who looks at a woman lustfully has already committed adultery with her in his heart.29 If your right eye causes you to stumble, gouge it out and throw it away. It is better for you to lose one part of your body than for your whole body to be thrown into hell. 30 And if your right hand causes you to stumble, cut it off and throw it away. It is better for you to lose one part of your body than for your whole body to go into hell.

Matthew 5:27–30

4. McDowell, Josh, *Givers Takers & Other Kinds of Lovers*, p.52

What was Jesus saying here? Firstly, as we noted with the commandment forbidding murder, he was suggesting that the act of adultery begins long before there is any physical touch. The outward action is merely the final stage of a sin which has been developing in the heart or mind of a person. To look lustfully upon another person, from God's perspective, is effectively the same as taking them to bed and having sex with them.

Meeting someone and experiencing a sense of physical attraction (which to a certain extent is normal or natural), develops into lust as thoughts dwelled upon in the mind awaken sexual drives toward that person. This imagination may then be fed with fantasies of sexual play. Entertaining of such lustful thoughts and fantasies are no different, according to Jesus, to committing adultery with that person.

It is not hard to imagine the impact of what Jesus was saying on his original congregation—many of whom had possibly been feeling comfortable and perhaps even proud of being guilt-free with respect to physical adultery. Undoubtedly, there were more people feeling guilty after Jesus expanded the definition of adultery in this way. Chances are many of us, when we apply this definition, will realize that we have also been tripped up by the sin of adultery.

The second thing Jesus said was even more radical, as it addresses our response to this kind of temptation:

> If your right eye causes you to stumble, gouge it out
> and throw it away . . . if your right hand causes you to
> stumble, cut it off and throw it away . . .

Now, what was Jesus suggesting here? Was he really talking about literal mutilation of one's body, as one young man did some years back when he emasculated himself in order to combat his problem with sexual fantasy! Is that what Jesus was commending or was he talking figuratively?

Obviously, Jesus wasn't talking about literally cutting off a hand or plucking out an eye. He was talking about removing the source of temptation. If there are certain things in a person's life that tend to cause them to sin or act like a stumbling block, they should be ruthless and cut those things out of their life.

The original Greek word translated in our English Bibles as "cause to sin" or in some translations "stumbling block," is an interesting word (*skandalethron*). It comes from a word which translates literally as "bait stick."[5] A bait stick was the stick or arm on which bait was fixed to lure an animal into a trap. For example, the stick with cheese on that, when the mouse stands on it, brings the trap down on its neck.

What Jesus was saying was quite simple: Get rid of the bait stick in your life. Destroy or remove from your life those things that are a lure toward temptation. In the same way as plucking out an eye or cutting off a hand is a ruthless radical action, likewise be ruthless and actively prune from your life those things that provide a source for temptation.

When Jesus talked about the eye and the hand he was probably tapping into a well-understood analogy amongst the Jews of his day. There was a saying amongst the Jewish Rabbis, "The eyes and the hands are the two brokers of sin."[6] The eye is the medium through which the temptation comes, and the hand is the instrument by which the action is committed. Both are key elements in sinning.

So, when Jesus talked about the sin of adultery he suggested that it was more than having sex with another man's wife or another woman's husband. The issue begins in one's mind, so the best way to respond is to look at the things in one's life that trip, trap or lure us to disobedience. When we spend time with some of our friends, do we find ourselves doing what we know to be wrong? Better to cut off that friendship and be lonely than to have lots of friends now but spend eternity in hell. Does our place of employment offer unreasonable risk of temptation? In the same way that it would be plain stupid for an alcoholic to get a job at a brewery or store that sells alcohol, might a person's employment provide an unreasonable lure toward corruption and sin? Wise up, better to be unemployed than to be gainfully employed in this life but spend

---

5. William Barclay, *The Daily Study Bible–The Gospel of Matthew Vol. 1*, p.148.

6. Ibid, p.147.

eternity in hell. If a person is bombarded with thoughts of sexual lust and perversion every time they surf the internet, better to cancel our internet account than have technology that provides quick access to media in this life and spend eternity in hell. If a person cannot control their thought life every time they go to the beach, and see women in skimpy bathing suits, maybe cut out going to the beach. Better to sacrifice one's suntan than to spend eternity roasting in hell.

A man regularly attended a prayer meeting at his church, and every time he would pray along the lines of, "Lord please clear away the cobwebs from our eyes and our lives." After hearing this man pray passionately like this for several months another person in the prayer meeting, in exasperation, finally blurted out, "Lord please kill the spider!"

When Jesus taught his disciples how to pray he encouraged them to include the request, "Lead us not into temptation." That's a good prayer to pray, but one wonders whether God sometimes feels like responding, "I'm not the one leading you into temptation . . . you're doing that well enough on your own!" In other words, rather than asking God to not lead us into temptation we need to take affirmative action and stop putting ourselves in a position where we can be tempted.

In concluding this chapter, a pastoral word to those who have "fallen" in areas of sexual sin. By Jesus' definition in his Sermon on the Mount, that possibly applies to us all. On the one hand, God holds a high moral standard for humanity, and those who disobey him become subject to his wrath and judgment. On the other hand, the Bible says that we are under judgement to the point that we confess and repent of our sin. When a person admits and turns away from their weakness, failure, and sin and toward God, he in his mercy extends forgiveness:

> 9 If we confess our sins, he is faithful and just and will forgive us our sins and purify us from all unrighteousness.
>
> 1 John 1:9

Herein is hope. If we have done this with respect to sexual sin, know that today we are free from the judgment of God. Any lingering guilt is false condemnation and comes from one source—the evil one.

Nevertheless, it may be that the physical consequences of a person's past sin continue, even though before God they are spiritually clean. Sexual sin often carries a consequence that isn't easy to escape. There may be physical results of sexual sin like pregnancy or disease. There may be emotional consequences such as damage to the trust and intimacy of a marriage relationship. Some of these things can take years to overcome and some of them are irreparable. A murderer, for instance, may well be forgiven by God for the sin of taking another person's life, but their sentence and debt to society still need to be served, and the impact for their victim is irreversible. Likewise, God may well have forgiven a sexual sinner and he or she is free in terms of their relationship with God, but the consequences of that sin on relationships with other people may not yet be healed. The sexual sinner must be willing to accept that consequence and not be impatient or demanding.

Likewise, a word to those who have never engaged in sexual sin in a physical sense: There is no place for a "tut-tut" attitude, where one looks down condescendingly or in judgment upon those who have sinned sexually. Before God, the sin of self-righteousness is just as serious as the sin of adultery. There but for the grace of God go we all!

For all Christ followers, allow the writer of Hebrews to have the last word:

> 4 Marriage should be honored by all, and the marriage bed kept pure, for God will judge the adulterer and all the sexually immoral.
>
> Hebrews 13:4

Small Group Discussion Questions

1. What do you think the average person in our country understands to be the attitude of God or the Bible toward sex? Why have they formed that conclusion?

2. Do you think the media merely reflects the prevailing attitude toward sexuality in our day and age, or does it more lead the way in how we think?

3. Given the fact that every one of us is the bi-product of a sexual act, why do you think Christians/churches don't talk much about sexuality? Is this good or bad?

4. How would you respond to the person who says that the traditional biblical view on sexuality inhibits freedom or restricts personal choice?

5. Why do you think the Bible makes such a big issue about sex?

6. What do you consider to be the teaching points from Paul's comments in 1 Corinthians 7:2–5?

7. How might the twenty-first-century Christian church apply the principle in Hebrews 13:4?

Chapter 8

To Catch A Thief

APPARENTLY BEING A THIEF does not require you to be the brightest light bulb in the chandelier! In fact, not being very clever might be a more typical qualification. For example, the man who walked into a bank and handed the teller a note demanding money. When he arrived home, he found the police waiting for him. The erstwhile bank robber had written the robbery note on his own deposit slip! The police simply went to his house and waited for him to return.

Then there were the two men who decided to steal an ATM machine from a shopping mall. They hooked up a chain around the machine and connected it to the bumper bar of their truck, intending to drag it home. However, they failed to consider how securely ATM machines are anchored to the wall. Rather than dislodging the ATM machine they ripped their bumper off. Afraid of being caught they took off down the road leaving the bumper behind. Unfortunately, they forgot that the license plate of the truck was still attached to the bumper identifying them as the owners of the vehicle.

The subject of stealing or theft is the focus of the eighth value statements that God gave to the newly forming nation of Israel. When it comes to the property and possessions of others there is a very clear, incontrovertible boundary for God's people:

15 You shall not steal.

Exodus 20:15

The taking, or misappropriation, of someone else's property or assets is expressly forbidden. It is unacceptable behavior. It is conduct that is in conflict with God's definition of justice and is not permitted among those who live within his Kingdom.

In the New Testament, it is a principle stated in unequivocal terms within a letter the Apostle Paul wrote to the Christians of Ephesus. It seems apparent that there must have been an issue needing to be addressed:

> 8 Those who have been stealing must steal no longer, but must work, doing something useful with their own hands, that they may have something to share with those in need.

Ephesians 4:28

Followers of Jesus Christ respect the property of others. If stealing is, or has been, an aspect of a person's lifestyle in the past, it is something they are to stop doing.

According to the Bible, there are only two ways by which a person can legitimately increase the property or possessions they own. The first is as a reward or in compensation for work that they perform. The person who works earns and deserves remuneration for that work, and from that remuneration, they are able to legitimately purchase goods and services. The person who does not work, or who is lazy, cannot expect to legitimately acquire additional possessions.

Apparently, this was an area where some of the early Christians needed to lift their game. For instance, Paul wrote to the Christians in the city of Thessalonica:

> 7 For you yourselves know how you ought to follow our example. We were not idle when we were with you, 8 nor did we eat anyone's food without paying for it. On the contrary, we worked night and day, laboring and toiling so that we would not be a burden to any of you . . . 10 For

even when we were with you, we gave you this rule: "The one who is unwilling to work shall not eat."

2 Thessalonians 3:7–8;10

The thief acquires property not by working but by stealing from others; in contrast, the righteous person acquires property by working hard to earn it.

The second way the Bible sanctions the acquisition of property and possessions is through a gift. Someone may give a gift directly so that the recipient benefits from the other's generosity or they may impart an inheritance and the beneficiary prospers as the result of that last will and testament. Their possessions increase, or they have extended capability to make purchases, through the generosity or benevolence of somebody else. They didn't earn it necessarily, but they also didn't steal it.

The person who acquires property other than through these two means does so in an unlawful manner. The thief takes the property, possessions, or wealth of someone without their permission, and without the fair exchange of work that might have earned them that income.

What is it that drives or motivates people to steal? Contrary to popular opinion, people who steal do not primarily come from the poorest sectors of society. A simple search on shoplifting statistics, for instance, suggests that only three percent of shoplifters are career criminals. Seventy-five percent of those who steal from shops or businesses are adults, and most are demographically middle-class and wealthy. Seventy-two percent of incidents occur without premeditation, and most offenders don't commit other types of crimes (For example, they will not steal an ashtray from another's house and will likely return a $20 bill that they see a person has dropped).[1] One new up-market hotel apparently reported that in the first 10 months of operation they lost: 38,000 pieces of cutlery, 18,000 towels, 355 silver coffeepots, 1,500 silver finger bowls, and 100 Bibles!

---

1. National Association for Shoplifting Prevention

The drive or motivation to steal seems to have much less to do with poverty or desperate lack, and much more to do with greed and selfishness. They refuse to live within their lawful means and greedily choose to add to it by stealing from others. G.K. Chesterton had good advice for those who are dissatisfied with what they currently have: "There are two ways to get enough. One is to continue to accumulate more; the other is to desire less." [2] A thief is characteristically a greedy person who generally wants more than they currently have.

For most people, this eighth commandment falls into the "clear and simple" category. Most people regard themselves as honest; they don't go around stealing things from other people. "What more is there to say? Let's move on to the next commandment." But are we as lily-white on this issue as we think we are?

For instance, the person who cheats on their tax filing is actually a thief. They defraud or steal from the government, or more particularly from the rest of their society. This might go down like the proverbial lead balloon, but the Bible actually encourages the payment of taxes! Remember that occasion when a group of Pharisees tried to trap Jesus over the issue of taxation? [3] The popular view was that paying tax to a corrupt government (in those days the Roman Empire) was something people should avoid wherever possible. In response Jesus made the famous statement: "Give to Caesar what is Caesar's and give to God what is God's."[4] In other words, the rule of law and societal governance, and provisions for freedom and justice in a society, are worthy of our financial support. Good citizens in a society have a moral responsibility to support the public purse. The person who dodges tax by declaring a less than honest account of their income, not only lies, but also steals from the rest of their community.

Some may be tempted to think this is making too strong a case from one little statement Jesus made, but apparently the

---

2. Chesterton, G.K, *The Crimes of England,* (A Word To The Wise, 2013)

3. Matthew 22:21; Mark 12:17; Luke 20:25

4. Matthew 22:21; Mark 12:17; Luke 20:25

Apostle Paul also thought it important. Here's what he suggested to the Christians living in the city of Rome:

> 6 This is also why you pay taxes, for the authorities are God's servants, who give their full time to governing. 7 Give to everyone what you owe them: If you owe taxes, pay taxes; if revenue, then revenue; if respect, then respect; if honor, then honor.

Romans 13:6–7

Everyone wants law and order, and the freedom to be able to travel safely around their community. Who pays police salaries? A good education is something everyone wants for our children. Who pays the teachers? A civil society provides a safety net for the poor, and medical services for the sick. Who pays the cost of hospitals and pensions? Likewise, safe roads, efficient waste management, and other community services are funded through our taxes. The person who lies or cheats on their tax return actually steals from our collective community purse.

Then there's the person who artificially inflates their reimbursement claim for a business trip—claiming personal expenses from their company that are beyond what is allowed. They've become a thief by taking property or wealth from their employer that they are not entitled to. Likewise, when an employee takes home stationery or business supplies meant for use in their office or factory or overstates tax deduction claims or uses a business phone for personal calls, they are all stealing. Some may attempt to justify their actions, saying that the company can afford it or won't miss it, but if a person takes from their employer beyond what has been negotiated in their remuneration package, the Bible declares them a thief. The eighth commandment has been broken.

Another way people steal from their employer in the workplace is by being late to work, slack in the performance of their duties or by calling in sick when they are not unwell. If payment is received for work that has not been performed and no attempt is made to rectify the overpayment, they're a thief. The Bible places a high value on personal integrity and diligence in the workplace.

What a person earns they should work for. As Paul told the Thessalonians:

> 11 We hear that some among you are idle. They are not busy; they are busybodies. 12 Such people we command and urge in the LORD Jesus Christ to settle down and earn the food they eat.
>
> 2 Thessalonians 3: 11–12

Flipping the employment coin over, the employer who does not pay his or her employees a wage that is proportionate to their labor is also a thief. The Bible instructs employers to treat their staff fairly and to reward them adequately for the labor they perform. There is actually a biblical warrant for something like a "living wage."

> 1And masters, treat your servants considerately. Be fair with them. Don't forget for a minute that you, too, serve a Master—God in heaven.
>
> Colossians 4:1 (The Message)

> 4 Look! The wages you failed to pay the workers who mowed your fields are crying out against you. The cries of the harvesters have reached the ears of the LORD Almighty.
>
> James 5:4

If people are employed, but not paid a fair wage, they have effectively been the victims of theft. Their employer has stolen from them what they were due.

Not "owning up" to damage done to another person's property is another form of theft. The dent put in the fender of a car in the supermarket carpark and not owned up to, or the tool borrowed and returned damaged without alerting its owner, are forms of theft. Likewise, knowingly selling a product or a commodity that is not fit for purpose or does not live up to the hype about it, is stealing. To knowingly sell a car that is defective, or a house that leaks or floods, and not disclose this, is a form of fraud. And fraud, according to the Bible, is a form of stealing.

11 Honest scales and balances are from the LORD; all the weights in the bag are of his making.

Proverbs 16:11

23 The LORD detests differing weights, and dishonest scales do not please him.

Proverbs 20:23

There is another form of theft of which we might be guilty—the Bible speaks of people stealing from God. The Prophet Malachi announced:

6 "I the LORD do not change. So you, the descendants of Jacob, are not destroyed. 7 Ever since the time of your ancestors you have turned away from my decrees and have not kept them. Return to me, and I will return to you," says the LORD Almighty.

But you ask, "How are we to return?"

8 'Will a mere mortal rob God? Yet you rob me.

But you ask, "How are we robbing you?"

"In tithes and offerings. 9 You are under a curse—your whole nation—because you are robbing me. 10 Bring the whole tithe into the storehouse, that there may be food in my house. Test me in this," says the LORD Almighty, "and see if I will not throw open the floodgates of heaven and pour out so much blessing that there will not be room enough to store it."

Malachi 3:6–10

The people of God worship him with their income. As an act of honoring God, they give to him:

9 Honor the LORD with your wealth, with the firstfruits of all your crops; 10 then your barns will be filled to over-flowing, and your vats will brim over with new wine.

Proverbs 3:9–10

It is one thing to steal from a fellow human being, but it raises the ante a little when a person steals from the Lord!

The more we stop and think about it, perhaps the less guiltless we might want to claim ourselves to be with respect to the eighth commandment. We may not have robbed a bank, or broken into a house and stole cash from the safe, but are there other ways that we have crossed the line and taken what is not rightfully ours?

It might even be argued that the person who refuses to witness to their experience of being a Christian is also a thief. They steal the hope of life and restored relationship with God from those amongst whom they have been "planted" in order to influence and demonstrate to them the truth of the gospel. They effectively steal another's opportunity for eternal life.

What does one do when they recognize that they are guilty of stealing? What remedial work can be done in response to a revelation about this aspect of one's character?

The short answer is to *stop doing it!* Make a conscious, calculated decision of the will to change your behavior. Perhaps previously there hadn't been a connection between their conduct and stealing, but having recognized that this is what they are doing, the first response is to take Paul's advice:

> 28 Those who have been stealing must steal no longer . . .
>
> Ephesians 4:28

However, the Christian response to recognizing sin is not merely to stop doing it. The Christian response includes *repentance*. The word repentance (*metanoia*), essentially means "change of mind." [5] A person intentionally stops going in one direction, turns around, and heads back in the opposite direction. Inherent in the meaning of repentance is the concept of *restitution*. To repent of sin against another is not merely to stop doing it. There is also an act of restoration for that which has been damaged or a wrong that has been done. If something has been taken there is the moral obligation to restore it or make some recompense that endeavors to make what is wrong, right.

5. Vine, W.E, *"An Expository Dictionary of New Testament Words,"* p.952

There is a classic example of repentance and restitution in the nineteenth chapter of Luke's biography on the life of Jesus. Jesus was passing through a town called Jericho, where a man called Zacchaeus wanted to see him. Zacchaeus was notable for two things. Firstly, he was very short, so because of the crowds gathered along the road, the only way he could see Jesus was to climb a tree. The second thing he was known for was his job with the Inland Revenue. He was a tax collector. Back then, (maybe as now!), no one particularly liked tax collectors. In Jesus' day, they were regarded as loathsome because they worked for the Romans. The Romans would tender out the contract of tax collecting to one of the locals, and the tax collector was permitted to add a premium for their expenses. Most tax collectors, and Zacchaeus was no exception, used to rip off or extort those from whom they collected tax. Perhaps instead of charging $50 they would charge $80 and pocket the change. Zacchaeus was a thief and had stolen vast amounts of money from people. But then he met Jesus and was totally converted; his life was radically changed. What does that mean for a thief? Zacchaeus offers a good example:

> 8 But Zacchaeus stood up and said to the LORD, "Look, LORD! Here and now I give half of my possessions to the poor, and if I have cheated anybody out of anything, I will pay back four times the amount."

Luke 19:8

Not only did he stop stealing, not only did he change his behavior in the future, he also sought to put right that which he had done wrong. He made costly restitution. In the process, he demonstrated the power of God to change lives.

A well-known preacher spoke on this subject, and after the service a man came to him and said, "Pastor, you have put me in a real fix. I've been stealing from my employer and I'm ashamed to tell him about it. You see, I am a boat builder and the man I work for is an unbeliever. I've often talked to him about Christ, but he only laughs at me. In my work expensive copper nails are used because they won't rust in water. I've been taking some of them home for a boat I am building in my backyard. I'm afraid if I were to tell my boss what I've done, and offer to pay for them, he will think I'm a hypocrite and I will never be able to witness to him about Christ again. However, my conscience is really bothered."

Some days later, when the man saw the preacher again, he told him what happened. "Pastor, I've settled that matter and I feel so relieved."

"What happened when you told your boss?" asked the minister.

"Oh, he looked at me intently and said, 'George I always thought you were a hypocrite but now I'm not so sure. Maybe there is something to your Christianity after all. Any religion that makes a man admit he has been stealing a few copper nails, and offer to settle for them, must be worth having.'"[6]

In closing this chapter, I would like to suggest one more way that some may be guilty of theft. So far, the concept of stealing from people, from employers and employees, from government and even from God, have been considered. But might some people also be guilty of stealing from themselves in terms of the rich potential God has deposited within them?

In the late 1880s in the United States there lived a man by the name of Emmanuel Ninger. The year he was caught stealing was 1887. He was in a neighborhood grocery store buying vegetables and paid with a $20 note. However, the shop teller noticed something odd. Her hands were wet from handling vegetables and when she took the $20 note she noticed that some of the ink was coming off on her hands. She looked at Emmanuel Ninger, who was both a friend and a neighbor, a man who had traded in the store for years, and she was puzzled. "Could this really be a counterfeit $20 note . . . from Emmanuel Ninger?" She quickly put the idea out of her mind. "Mr. Ninger would never do something like that." And she put the note in the drawer and gave him his change.

But when he left the store she took the $20 note out and had a closer look at it. In 1887 a $20 note was a lot of money. Although she knew who Emmanuel Ninger was, she figured it was too much money to gamble with and took it to the bank to authenticate.

6. Ironside,H.A, *Illustrations of Bible Truth*, p.104–106

Although it looked real, sure enough the ink rubbed off on your fingers.

Eventually, a search warrant was issued to search Emmanuel Ninger's home. To begin with, they found nothing in his house to implicate him, but then they climbed up into the attic. There they found what they were looking for; apparatus for producing counterfeit $20 notes. They were very simple: an easel, some paper, a paintbrush, and some paint. You see, Emmanuel Ninger was a gifted artist—absolutely brilliant! Meticulously, stroke by stroke, he was painting $20 notes by hand. However, Emmanuel Ninger was also a thief. He was arrested, tried and sent to jail for manufacturing counterfeit currency.

There is another little twist, though, to the story of Emmanuel Ninger. When the authorities searched the attic of his house they also found three amazing portraits that he had painted. At public auction sometime later those three paintings sold for a little over $16,000. Here's the irony of the story. It took Emmanuel Ninger about the same time to paint a counterfeit $20 note as it did to paint a beautiful portrait worth around $5000. [7]

Emmanuel Ninger was a thief alright. He was stealing from people by producing and passing off counterfeit currency. But he was also a person who had the potential to make a tremendous contribution to the world in which he lived. He had amazing talent and skill as an artist, and the personal wealth he might have accumulated from his work was incredible, but he aimed his talents in another direction. Emmanuel Ninger was a thief . . . who was stealing from himself!

7. Ziglar Zig, *Sermon Illustrations-Stealing*

Small Group Discussion Questions

1. What experience(s) have you had of having something stolen from you? How did it make you feel?

2. What experience(s) have you had (in your pre-Christians days, of course!) of stealing? What was your motivation at the time?

3. What are some examples of stealing or theft that have virtually become a part of our contemporary culture?

4. People who shoplift are not necessarily poor. Why do you think people who can afford to buy goods steal them?

5. Repentance from our sin often requires restoration and restitution. What about situations where that cannot be done?

6. What challenge does Luke 19:8 bring to your situation?

7. What will you do differently this week for considering the eighth commandment?

Chapter 9

Tell the Truth, the Whole Truth, and Nothing but the Truth

A PASTOR CONCLUDED HIS sermon with the announcement that next Sunday he was going to preach on lying and dishonesty. He asked his congregation if they would do some homework during the intervening week and come back to church on Sunday having read the seventeenth chapter of the Gospel of Mark. The next Sunday the pastor began his sermon with the question, "Would all of you who did as I requested last Sunday, and read Mark 17, please raise your hand?"

Nearly every hand in the congregation went up. "Very good," said the pastor. "You are precisely the people I wish to speak to this morning. There are only sixteen chapters in the book of Mark!"

In 1993, the Port Authority of New York and New Jersey ran an advertisement for electricians in the "Situations Vacant" section of the local newspaper and specified that only those who had experience with *Sontag* connectors should apply. They received 170 responses from electricians claiming to be proficient with *Sontag* componentry. However, there was apparently no such thing as *Sontag* connectors. The Human Resources department within the

Port Authority had simply run the advertisement to see how many people falsified their resume when applying for jobs. [1]

The subject of this chapter is truthfulness. What we say and the impression we convey need to be absolutely true, or else we are lying, and lying is conduct that falls outside of God's boundaries. Speaking anything other than the truth is forbidden behavior. The ninth commandment reads:

> 16 You shall not give false testimony against your neighbor
>
> Exodus 20:16

For the follower of Jesus, their character and words are to be true, honest, believable and dependable.

The Bible has a huge amount to say about honesty. In fact, truth is one of the central pillars of Christian belief and philosophy. Jesus claimed to be the personification of truthfulness when he said: "I am the way, the truth, and the life . . . " [2] Christianity is founded on truth. A truth that Jesus said sets people free from captivity to all manner of bondage and enslavement. So, the issue of being truthful, of not lying with our mouth, is highly valued amongst God's people.

When God gave Moses his laws for the emerging Jewish nation 3500 years ago, the imperative to speak truthfully was a crucial foundation in their system of justice. Indeed, a person could be found guilty of a crime only on the testimony of two or more truth-speaking witnesses:

> 15 One witness is not enough to convict anyone accused of any crime or offense they may have committed. A matter must be established by the testimony of two or three witnesses.
>
> Deuteronomy 19:15

1. Wexler, Mark N. , *"Successful Resume Fraud: Conjectures on the Origins of Amorality in the Workplace,"* p.137–152

2. John 14:6

There were special punishments set aside for (malicious) witnesses who did not tell the truth, the whole truth, and nothing but the truth:

> 16 If a malicious witness takes the stand to accuse someone of a crime, 17 the two people involved in the dispute must stand in the presence of the LORD before the priests and the judges who are in office at the time. 18 The judges must make a thorough investigation, and if the witness proves to be a liar, giving false testimony against a fellow Israelite, 19 then do to the false witness as that witness intended to do to the other party. You must purge the evil from among you. 20 The rest of the people will hear of this and be afraid, and never again will such an evil thing be done among you.
>
> Deuteronomy 19:16–20

Being less than honest was regarded as a serious crime. The perjurer or liar received the same punishment as the accused person. A similar principle applies in the systems of jurisprudence within most countries today. To lie in a court of law, or to make a spurious accusation to the police, is a serious offense.

A few hundred years later, the book of Proverbs offered a commentary on the consequences of deceit:

> 9 With their mouths the godless destroys their neighbors.
>
> Proverbs 11:9

> 4 A wicked person listens to deceitful lips; a liar pays attention to a destructive tongue.
>
> Proverbs 17:4

> 5 A false witness will not go unpunished, and whoever pours out lies will not go free.
>
> Proverbs 19:5

> 18 Like a club or a sword or a sharp arrow is the one who gives false testimony against a neighbor.
>
> Proverbs 25:18

Jesus also had strong words to say about truthfulness in one's speech. In Matthew 15:19 he connects giving false testimony and lying together with crimes like murder, adultery, theft, and sexual immorality. In the eyes of Jesus, being untruthful is not an insignificant matter. In John 8, Jesus identified deceitful speech as the devil's language:

> 44 . . . he was a murderer from the beginning, not holding to the truth, for there is no truth in him. When he lies, he speaks his native language, for he is a liar and the father of lies.
>
> John 8:44

While being multi-lingual and able to communicate in several languages is commendable, there is one language we ought not to become proficient in—the devil's native language of lying.

Later in the New Testament era, when Paul wrote to the Ephesian believers he had this to say about honesty in our speech:

> 25 Therefore each of you must put off falsehood and speak truthfully to your neighbor, for we are all members of one body
>
> Ephesians 4:25

When people are less than truthful they undermine the foundations of community, for community and fellowship are built upon trust, and trust is founded on truthfulness.

In exploring the implications of the ninth commandment a question worth investigating might be, why do people give false testimony against their neighbor? What motivates people to be deceitful or economical with the truth? There are several motivations, but perhaps the most serious is *malice*—the desire to cause someone else hurt or harm. People lie or spread a false report to get someone else into trouble, or as a spiteful act of vengeance. With their tongue, and a few choice words, they intentionally, perhaps maliciously, cause grief or pain to someone who has offended them. Telling an untruth has been likened to a long-range weapon. To physically attack, a person needs to be in close proximity to their victim. However, with an untruthful comment or rumor, a person can attack someone from the other side of the world!

Then there are some people who lie because they are *selfish* and *greedy*. They play fast and loose with the truth for their own self-centered comfort. This conduct is reflected in the story of a grumpy old man who boarded a train and occupied the best seat in a small cabin. He then tried to reserve the adjacent seat for himself as well, by placing his luggage upon it. Just before the crowded train began to move from the station a teenage boy came running up and jumped aboard. "This car is full," said the old man irritably. "That seat next to me is reserved for a friend of mine who has put his bag there." The young man paid no attention to what was said and simply replied, "Alright, I'll just stay here until he comes," whereupon he sat himself down on the seat and placed the suitcase upon his lap while the elderly man glared at him with contempt. Of course, the old man's "friend" didn't appear and soon the train began to move. As it glided past the platform the young man tossed the bag through the open window remarking, "Apparently your friend missed his train. We can't let him lose his luggage too!"

There are other people who lie for *fear* or out of *self-preservation*. Perhaps they have been caught doing something they know is wrong and they tell a lie to try and get out of it. That is arguably the cause of the very first lie recorded in the Bible; when Adam was confronted by God for his disobedience over eating forbidden fruit in the Garden of Eden, he bent the truth and blamed his wife!

Another primary motive for lying is for gain or *personal profit*. People misrepresent the truth to make money. Like the story of the farmer who took his horse to see the vet. He complained about his horse: "One day he limps, the next day he doesn't. What should I do?"

The vet responded: "On the day he doesn't limp, sell him!"

There are many reasons why people misrepresent the truth. Some people do it compulsively, some habitually, some as a manner of casual speaking. Do a simple search on the internet for common lies that people tell, and numerous lists and examples are suggested. For example, the *Top Ten Liar's Casual Lies*—most people can identify with some:

10. We'll stay only five minutes . . .

9. This will be a short meeting . . .

8. I'll respect you in the morning . . .

7. The check is in the mail . . .

6. I'm from the government and I'm here to help you . . .

5. This hurts me more than it hurts you . . .

4. Your money will be cheerfully refunded . . .

3. We service what we sell . . .

2. Your table will be ready in just a minute . . .

1. I'll start exercising/dieting tomorrow . . .

Perhaps this raises another question, when is a lie really a lie? The focus of the ninth commandment is quite specific. Its legal term today is perjury. A person is asked to give testimony about their neighbor, and in doing so provides misinformation. As already noted, misrepresenting the truth when called as a witness in a court of law is a serious offense.

But there are a host of other ways that the ninth commandment is broken, because the principle behind it surely applies to any situation where a person knowingly misleads people. From the words that are said (or written), do others gain an understanding or an impression of someone, or something, or some situation that is different to what the person providing the information knows to be true? Giving false testimony against a neighbor applies to many things.

Slander is a form of lying. When false statements are made that injure another person's character or reputation the ninth commandment is broken. Never under-estimate the power of the tongue or the destructive force of a rumor. There is a famous story of a town gossip who consulted with her counselor and half-heartedly said she would like to make amends for the stories she had spread throughout the town. The counselor said he knew a way that she could do it. He instructed her to pick two handfuls of ripe dandelions and walk through the town holding them high and letting the wind carry the seeds. Upon completion of her task, she returned to the counselor. He then told her to retrace her steps and gather up all the seeds that she had strewn throughout the town. Aghast, the woman replied that this was impossible. There was no way she could pick up all those seeds. The counselor looked her squarely in the eye and said that it would be easier to gather the seeds of those plants than the seeds of her gossip and lies!

Another form of deceitful slander is to *insinuate* something about someone else that cannot be substantiated. One doesn't have to outright state something that is untrue, a subtler way is to say something that is open to interpretation or speculation. In recent years the bullying power of the 140-character *tweet* has become commonplace. It is used with great effect by politicians and political parties. Words used don't have to be explicitly untrue, instead they paint a picture in the mind of the reader. The truth can be misrepresented by being economical about what is conveyed. A person may not say something that is blatantly a lie, but by what they say, or don't say, have they conveyed an accurate impression of reality?

While they obviously didn't have social media in Jesus' day, there were times when those opposing him realized they couldn't stand up to Jesus' teaching or his power, so they muttered loudly and planted the idea amongst people that perhaps he came from a dubious background given those he liked to spend time with. They didn't say anything up front, they merely insinuated.[3]

Taking this a step further, another form of misrepresenting the truth might be by *not saying anything at all*. Being or bearing false witness can happen as much by what a person *doesn't* say, as by what they *do* say. There is such a thing as the lie of omission. A well-known pastor told the story of a woman in his church who was married for only a short time before she found out her husband was a homosexual and didn't want to be in a heterosexual

3. Luke 5:30; 15:2

marriage. Soon after the husband's disclosure, he left her. As the pastor talked with the devastated young woman she said something he would never forget. She said, "After I was divorced several of my friends came to me and said that they knew he was gay. When I asked them why they didn't say anything to me they said, 'We didn't think it was any of our business.'" In other words, the husband had been dishonest or confused about his sexual orientation, but this young woman's supposed friends had perpetuated that deceit by remaining silent—most probably because it was the easy way out for them.

Interestingly, the idea of a person not speaking up when they know something that their neighbor should be made aware of, and refusing to do so, was something the ancient Law of Moses took seriously. It was a significant crime:

> If you sin by not stepping up and offering yourself as a witness to something you've heard or seen in cases of wrongdoing, you'll be held responsible.
>
> Leviticus 5:1 (The Message)

Lying is not merely the words a person speaks. It is also the impression that they convey.

Another subtle form of lying is *exaggeration*. Or as someone expressed it, "Some people don't mean to exaggerate—they just remember big!" They report the facts *"evang-elastically."* Maybe this is a sin pastors are prone to when they go to conferences and are asked how things are going back in their church, and they stretch the numbers and skew the statistics to make themselves look better. Whenever a person paints a picture that isn't true, they tell a lie.

Perhaps another subtle form of lying is *flattery*—giving compliments that we don't mean. For fear of hurting a sensitive person's feeling or perhaps receiving an unpleasant reaction, a person is told to their face something that is quite different to what might be said behind their back. "You sang beautifully," when it really wasn't that great. "I love your hairstyle" or "That was delicious," when it was awful. It's nice to be kind to people and being courteous and gracious is a good thing, but if what a person says is not the truth they become a false witness.

There is a delightful story about an elderly and wealthy countess who was very happy with her personal chauffeur. He was courteous, prompt, and efficient. The only complaint she had concerned his personal appearance. One day she said to him very diplomatically, "Randall how frequently do you think one should shave in order to look neat and proper?"

"Well madam," said Randall, who was also trying to be diplomatic, "with a light beard like yours, I'd say every three or four days would be enough!"

As might be expected, when it comes to the words people speak, Jesus offered timeless words of wisdom. In his Sermon on the Mount, in the context of swearing an oath, or making a solemn promise that was truthful and binding, Jesus talked specifically about retaining integrity in our spoken words. The cultural nuances here might be a little strange to a twenty-first-century worldview, but in the culture of Jesus' day, a kind of hierarchy had developed in the minds of many concerning statements made under oath. Certain oaths or promises were regarded as more binding than others. Here's what Jesus had to say:

> 33 'Again, you have heard that it was said to the people long ago, "Do not break your oath, but fulfil to the LORD the oaths you have made." 34 But I tell you, do not swear an oath at all: either by heaven, for it is God's throne; 35 or by the earth, for it is his footstool; or by Jerusalem, for it is the city of the Great King. 36 And do not swear by your head, for you cannot make even one hair white or black. 37 All you need to say is simply "Yes," or "No"; anything beyond this comes from the evil one.

Matthew 5:33–37

There was an unfortunate perception that certain promises could be wriggled out of depending on the nature of the oath. There were a couple of ways this kind of thing happened. There was what might be called *frivolous* swearing of an oath, where it wasn't really necessary.[4] To give a couple of twenty-first-century equivalents, maybe something like, "In the name of God I promise to buy a gallon of milk on my way home from work tonight . . ." or "As God is my judge, I will mow the lawns on Saturday afternoon . . ." The making of an oath was simply unnecessary and had the effect of cheapening those occasions when a formal declaration of promise was appropriate.

Then there was what might be called *evasive* swearing.[5] The idea behind this was that if a person invoked the name of God to convince others that a statement was true, or that a promise was binding, it carried more weight. God was somehow part of the equation. But other oaths, that invoked the "earth" or "heaven" or "Jerusalem" or one's "head," had more wriggle room. They weren't deemed to be quite so binding.

A similar hierarchy of truthfulness exists in the contemporary culture. We talk about "white lies" being acceptable. Or a witness in a court of law promises to tell the truth, the whole truth, and nothing but the truth, with their hand placed on a Bible, as if this will ensure the veracity of their statements. Then there are phrases that are used like, "As God is my witness . . ."

In the culture of Jesus' day, the measure of honesty and integrity had become a little ambiguous. Jesus' response to this was simple—swearing an oath ought to be totally unnecessary. He said: "Let your yes be yes, and your no, no." In other words, be people of your word. What a person says must always be honest and true, and what a person says they will do they must always do. Any need for divine attestation or additional reinforcement is then totally redundant.

Or as C.S. Lewis is reputed to have once said, "A little lie is like a little pregnancy. It doesn't take long before everyone knows!" [6]

---

4. William Barclay, *The Daily Study Bible-The Gospel of Matthew Vol. 1*, p.159.

5. Ibid, p.159.

6. Lewis, C.S., *AZ Quotes*

Small Group Discussion Questions

1. What is the worst lie you have ever told (in your pre-Christian days, of course!)?

2. What is the effect of lying? What damage does it do?

3. When is a lie a lie? Are there situations where it is permissible to bend the truth?

4. What are the implications from Leviticus 5:1? Where might this principle find application in our twenty-first-century context?

5. How have you been impacted by lying in the form of slander or insinuation?

6. How can you put into practice the teaching of Jesus in Matthew 5:33–37?

7. What will you do differently this week for considering this ninth commandment?

Chapter 10

The Law of Enough

ON THE 16 NOVEMBER 1930, Mrs. Henrietta Garret, a lonely 81-year-old widow, died in her home in Philadelphia and unwittingly started the most fantastic case of inheritance litigation in human history. She failed to leave a will, or at least no will could be found, for the disposal of her $17 million estate—a mystery that remains unsolved. She had expertly handled her financial affairs since her husband's death in 1895, and many felt that she must have realized that without a will her fortune would become the focus of legal battles among potential heirs.

At the time of her death, Mrs. Garret had only one known relative, a second cousin, and less than a dozen friends. Attempts to prove a relationship to her, and therefore claim a part of her estate, was made by more than 26,000 people from forty-seven states throughout America and twenty-nine foreign countries, represented by more than 3,000 lawyers. In their efforts to obtain a share of her estate people committed perjury, faked family records, changed their own names, altered family Bibles and concocted absurd tales of illegitimacy. As a result, twelve people were confined to psychiatric institutions, ten received jail sentences, two committed suicide and three were murdered. [1]

---

1. Ken Trivette, Sermonsearch-*The Sin That Nobody Confesses as Sin*

Perhaps all of them were guilty of breaking the tenth commandment!

As noted, Israel had only recently begun its journey toward nationhood and God presented them with ten value statements or moral boundaries within which they were to live. The first four dealt with their relationship with God and how his people ought to order their lives around him as the center of their being. The remaining six commandments related to how his people were to treat and interact with others in their community and outside of it.

The tenth commandment is about an insidious disease of the human heart that is highly infectious. Unless specific steps are taken to avoid it, it is a condition just about everybody contracts at some stage or other.

> 17 You shall not covet your neighbor's house. You shall not covet your neighbor's wife, or his male or female servant, his ox or donkey, or anything that belongs to your neighbor.
>
> Exodus 20:17

It has been suggested that the tenth commandment is the subtlest of them all, and that it's probably the one least owned up to, because evidence of its infringement is difficult to substantiate. The other nine commandments leave a trail of evidence. It is possible to observe and often prove when a person is lying, stealing, committing adultery, murdering, or dishonoring their parents. You can hear a person take the Lord's name in vain or watch them bow down to a false god. But when it comes to coveting the evidence is much less visible. It affects the thoughts and ambitions of a person in the secrecy of their mind, and there is often no external evidence to be noticed.

What exactly is meant by the word, "covet?" It is not a word used a lot in our everyday language. Some English translations have used alternatives like "desire" or "envy" to try and convey the intent of this commandment.

Literally, the English word "covet" means to "deeply desire something that you do not have." In the New Testament, the Greek word Paul used (*epithumeó*) could be rendered as "to desire or lust after." [2] A pure translation of the original Hebrew word might be "to desire or pant after or take pleasure in" [3] something.

In short, to covet something that belongs to someone else is to deeply desire it. A desire that can grow within a person to the point that they simply must have or acquire it regardless of cost or consequence. Our neighbor perhaps has a nicer house, a prettier wife, or a bunch of gadgets and toys that make us feel that what we have is inferior, when we covet these things we want them to such an extent that our perspective is lost. Coveting often leads to thought processes and behavior that are out of character. People who covet may do things they would never have thought themselves capable of doing, in order to get what they want.

Many household pets, it might be said, frequently transgress the tenth commandment. If their owners eat their meal before they have been fed, they look intently at their masters, salivating and cocking their head to the side, wondering when tit-bits of food might come their way!

Of course, it needs to be acknowledged that in the "developed" world coveting is probably what keeps the national economy ticking over. Every day, our household letterboxes, newsfeeds, and social media platforms are stuffed full of promotional advertisements—new toys and gimmicks, clothes and gadgets, that need to be purchased. The lure to covet is not discreet or subdued, it is flagrant and in our faces all the time. Perhaps one of the best commentaries on the pervasiveness of our coveting culture was a *Dennis the Menace* cartoon, where Dennis was looking through a catalog of toys and finally said, "This catalog has got a lot of toys I didn't even know I wanted!"

Perhaps that raises the question, "What's so wrong with wanting to acquire more things and possessions in life?" Why would God set in place a life value that warns people against the desire for more?

The answer to that question has to do with human greed. There is arguably nothing wrong *per se* with people increasing the

2. W.E. Vine, *"An Expository Dictionary of New Testament Words,"* p.244

3. Bible Hub, *Strongs Concordance*

number of possessions they own. To be rich or to own a lot of nice things is not inherently wrong or sinful. The issue with coveting is not about acquiring more, it's about the hunger for more which can become an insatiable desire. It can become a thirst that cannot be quenched or a hunger that cannot be satisfied.

In Ecclesiastes 5:10 Solomon made a comment about the human heart:

> 10 Whoever loves money never has enough; whoever loves wealth is never satisfied with their income . . .

When a person sees what their neighbor has, and desires it for themselves, it is not a finite emotion. When a person gets what they desperately wanted they typically still don't feel satisfied. It is like an addiction to a drug. Having satisfied one craving they invariably see something else, and the desire within them groans once more to possess it.

Flip this tenth commandment *coin* over to the other side, and another way of describing this life-value might be, "The Law of Enough." The opposite of coveting and greed for more is satisfaction with what one currently has. The person who covets his/her neighbor's house, or spouse, or servant, or tools, is a person dissatisfied with what they currently have. People who constantly want or pant for money and possessions frequently fall into a trap that eventually destroys them.

In Luke's biography on the life of Jesus, he records a brief discussion that Jesus had with a man in a dispute with his brother over an inheritance. The man wanted Jesus to arbitrate. Note how Jesus replied.

> 14 Jesus replied, 'Man, who appointed me a judge or an arbiter between you?' 15 Then he said to them, 'Watch out! Be on your guard against all kinds of greed; life does not consist in an abundance of possessions.'
>
> Luke 12:14–15

The culture of our world tells us that the way to be happy and fulfilled in life is to be rich and prosperous. The ability to buy whatever we want, whenever we want it, is presented as a benchmark for happiness. By contrast, Jesus said that in the culture of God's kingdom, being rich and prosperous isn't important. In fact, being greedy for more is a subtle and dangerous trap.

The Apostle Paul put it more directly in his first letter to Timothy:

> 9 Those who want to get rich fall into temptation and a trap and into many foolish and harmful desires that plunge people into ruin and destruction. 10 For the love of money is a root of all kinds of evil. Some people, eager for money, have wandered from the faith and pierced themselves with many griefs.
>
> 1 Timothy 6: 9–10

Chasing after wealth and prosperity has led to the downfall of many people. Over the last six or seven decades many preachers have told the story of a high-powered meeting in 1923, held at the Edgewater Beach Hotel in Chicago. Attending this meeting were nine of the world's most successful financiers of the time. There was: the president of the largest independent steel company (Charles M. Schwab), the president of the largest utility company (Samuel Insull), the president of the largest gas company (Howard Hospson), the greatest wheat speculator (Arthur Cutten), the president of the New York Stock Exchange (Richard Whitney), a member of the President's Cabinet (Albert Fall), and the president of the Bank of International Settlements (Leon Fraser). It was a meeting of some of the world's most successful men—at least men who had found the secret of making money.

However, twenty-five years later a different story is true of these men. Charles Schwab died bankrupt and lived on borrowed money for five years before his death. Samuel Insull died a fugitive from justice and penniless in a foreign land. Howard Hospson suffered mental illness and was declared insane. Arthur Cutten died abroad, insolvent. Richard Whitney spent many years in Sing Sing Penitentiary. Albert Fall, committed suicide, as did Leon Fraser.

Evidently, while all these men learned well the art of making money, none of them learned how to live.[4]

Surely none would argue with the assertion that in our own age, many people seem to worship money and/or what it can buy. So much so, that for many the Lord's Prayer has been subtly rewritten,

> "Our dollar who art invested
> Hallowed be our capital gains
> Thy dividends come
> Thy compounding be done
> In stocks as it is in bonds.
> Give us this day our daily interest
> And forgive us our debts
> As we have not forgiven our debtors
> And do not lead us into recession
> But deliver us from double-digit inflation
> For thine is the kingdom, and the power and the glory
> For now.
> Amen"[5]

The opposite of greed and coveting after a neighbor's possessions is contentment. Being satisfied with what we currently have, and being content, is again a subject about which the Bible has a lot to say. Previously we looked at Paul's words to Timothy about people wanting to get rich and falling into temptation and ruin. Immediately prior to that statement Paul had this to say:

> 6 But godliness with contentment is great gain. 7 For we brought nothing into the world, and we can take nothing out of it. 8 But if we have food and clothing, we will be content with that.
>
> 1 Timothy 6: 6–8

4. cf. https://www.snopes.com/glurge/fortune.asp for further information concerning the veracity of this story, along with research on the actual fate of these successful businessmen.

5. Original source unknown

When the Apostle Paul wrote to the Philippian Church he said:

> 11 . . . I have learned to be content whatever the circum-
> stances 12 . . . I have learned the secret of being content
> in any and every situation whether well fed or hungry,
> whether living in plenty or in want.

Philippians 4: 11–12

Satisfaction or contentment in life for Paul was not equated with his income or the level of comfort in which he lived. Indeed, when Paul wrote this statement about being content his "home" at the time was a prison. One doesn't imagine prison food or conditions in those days were much to write home about, and there wouldn't have been a great deal of exciting entertainment to fill his days, let alone improve his physical condition. Yet Paul was satisfied and content. Not because he possessed much in this world, but because of his relationship with Jesus.

In Luke 3 we read some challenging words from the mouth of John the Baptist about being content. There were many people responding to John's evangelistic ministry beside the Jordan River, and enquiring of him what they should do in order to demonstrate their repentance. At one point a group of soldiers asked him what they should do:

> 14 . . . He replied, "Don't extort money and don't accuse
> people falsely—be content with your pay."

Luke 3:14

Now, there's a challenge to our worldview that floats like the proverbial lead balloon! How many people would admit to being content with their pay? Doesn't everyone crave or lust or pant or covet for more in their pay-packet?

Jesus spoke about being content in Matthew 6:25–34, when he pointed our attention to the birds of the air that don't sow or reap or store their food away in barns, and yet they are fed by their Heavenly Father every day. He also suggested we look at the lilies of the field that don't fret or worry about how they will clothe themselves, and still their Heavenly Father adorns them beautifully.

"How much more," Jesus said, "will God do for his people whom he loves."

That's a theme that the writer of the book of Hebrews picked up.

> 5 Keep your lives free from the love of money and be content with what you have, because God has said, "Never will I leave you; never will I forsake you."
>
> Hebrews 13:5

Christians are very familiar with the idea of God's constant presence, they are convinced that he will never leave or forsake them. These were after all among the last words of Jesus (Matthew 28), just before he ascended into heaven. They are part of the *Great Commission,* an assurance which Jesus gave his followers as they went forth to make disciples of all nations.

Though actually, they go back much further. They resonate with a promise God gave the children of Israel in Deuteronomy 31:6. just before the Israelites crossed the Jordan River and entered the land of Canaan. These were very uncertain times for the Israelites, and there was a great deal of anxiety as to whether they would survive what lay ahead of them. They had been traveling for forty years toward the land God had promised them, and they knew it was good and fertile. The problem was the people who currently occupied that land liked it too! And they weren't looking to leave anytime soon. Acquiring their promised land would require a series of battles and struggles, and the people were understandably nervous. In response, God assured them that they were not going into the future alone. He would be with them every step of the way—both protecting and providing for their needs.

So, the crime of coveting or longing to have all that a neighbor has might not just be about being greedy; it may even be an insult that flies in the face of God. The person who constantly looks over the fence at what their neighbor has, and longs for those same things, is implying that God's supply of their needs is not enough. They are impugning his competence. They are disputing his wisdom and claiming that his provision is insufficient and needs to be supplemented.

To covet is fundamentally a slap in the face of God. A person is saying, in effect, that they know more than he does about how they should be provided for. Is that really something that we would want to do?

What can be done about all of this? If a person recognizes that, perhaps, they are guilty of breaking the tenth commandment, what remedial action could they take to repent of this kind of behavior? No doubt there are many steps that can be taken, but here are four specific actions that might curb coveting as part of our lifestyle:

1. Become habitually thankful

Take a good look at what we have already and give thanks to God for it. A person's home may not be in the flashiest of streets or furnished as nicely as those in a glossy magazine, but in most cases, we do have a roof over our heads. That is worth being grateful for. In its more sinister form, coveting is the fruit of an ungrateful heart. God is already with us in everything we face; spending time thanking him for what we have already is a great antidote to our craving after what another has.

2. Develop a realistic worldview

Perhaps more correctly, a literal worldview. See the whole world that God sees, not just the culture that we are a part of. Maybe a good investment towards anti-coveting behavior might be to take a trip through a "two-thirds-world" nation. There is something about seeing the plight of the *really* poor in this world that cures the selfish hearts of the rich, who whine and pine for more. One wonders how God handles it all; listening to the complaining and "first-world" frustrations of the comparatively wealthy, as they get hot and bothered over a worn-out lounge suite, a stained piece of carpet, or a scratch on their car; while other people in God's world appeal to him for a mud hut, a thatch roof, and just one meal a day. Do the things that worry and annoy us sometimes make God cross? Being aware of, and engaged with helping, the poor is a good way of curing a self-centered coveting attitude.

3. Check out of Christmas greed

The typical western celebration of Christmas has very little to do with the Christian faith from which it originated. Christmas in Western countries is appallingly focused on consumption, fueled by greed and covetousness. But don't blame the retail industry, they have simply tapped into the heart of the culture and fed people's desire for more and more of what they see their neighbor already has.

A lot of people have forgotten that Christmas greed is not actually compulsory! People are not compelled to celebrate Christmas the way everyone else does. It can be done very simply, at low cost, and in the process teach families the real meaning of God's gift of love—Jesus. It is perfectly possible to opt out of commercial Christmas greed. All it takes is a decision of the will not to behave in a non-Christian way. Everybody else in the street may lust and covet their neighbors' toys, but the good news is we don't have to compete with them in order to know real joy at Christmas. It's all about the choices that people make.

4. Trade down!

A lot of families in our community live beyond their means. Their chosen lifestyle is not affordable on their current income. Their mortgage is too high, the interest on their car loan is crippling, their credit card is maxed out. Why do people live like this and get themselves so crazily burdened with debt?

A large part of the reason has to do with their disobedience to the tenth commandment. Their neighbor has a pool, so they must have one. Their neighbor buys a new car, so they must upgrade theirs. They see their neighbor having a new lounge suite, a new fridge, or new TV delivered, and they must keep pace. And so, the debt-burden rises with each unrealistic loan agreement signed.

If a household has difficulty meeting their expenses, the first answer is quite simple. Trade down! Don't lust after all the new toys your neighbor has. Buy second-hand if new cannot be afforded. Stop competing with others and live within your means. Simplify the noise and clutter within your household.

There's a delightful fable about the man who lived in a tiny hut with his wife, two children, and his elderly parents. He tried to be patient and gracious but in desperation he consulted the village wise man.

"Do you have a rooster?" asked the wise man.

"Yes," he replied.

"Keep the rooster in the hut with your family and come and see me again next week."

The next week the man returned and told the wise elder that living conditions were worse than ever with the rooster crowing and making a mess of the hut. "Do you have a cow?" asked the wise elder. The man nodded fearfully. "Take your cow into the hut as well, then come and see me in a week."

Over the next several weeks the man, on the advice of the wise elder, made room for a goat, two dogs, and his brother's children. Finally, he could take it no more and in a fit of anger kicked out all the animals and guests leaving only his wife, his children, and his parents. The home suddenly became spacious and quiet and everyone lived happily ever after!

If a household is under financial stress, there are potentially two simple solutions:

1. Work harder

2. Live more simply.

Keeping the tenth commandment is more akin to the second solution.

A closing quotation from Alexander Solzhenitsyn, who offers excellent advice for those who look at what the neighbors have and wish it for themselves:

> "Do not pursue what is illusionary—property and position: all that is gained at the expense of your nerves decade after decade, and is confiscated in one fell night. Live with a steady superiority over life—don't be afraid of misfortune and do not yearn after happiness. It is, after all, all the same. The bitter doesn't last forever, and the sweet never fills the cup to overflowing. It is enough if you don't freeze in the cold and if hunger and thirst don't claw at your sides. If your back isn't broken, if your feet can walk, if both arms work, if both eyes can see, and if both ears can hear, then whom should you envy? And why? How envy of others devours us most of all. Rub your eyes and purify your heart and prize above all else in the world those who love you and wish you well."[6]

6. Aleksandr Solzhenitsyn, *The Gulag Archipelago* 1918–1956, (Mass market Paperback, 1974)

Small Group Discussion Questions

1. What evidence is there that a person is breaking the tenth commandment—coveting?

2. What experience have you (or someone you know) had of wanting something so much that it altered your sense of perspective?

3. What do you consider to be God's view of people who have lots of things/wealth in life?

4. Is it a sin to be wealthy?

5. How would you explain 1 Timothy 6:10 to someone new to the Christian faith?

6. What is your definition of contentment?

7. How do you think Paul was able to be content in a Philippian jail (Philippians 4:11,12)

8. What application do you take from Hebrews 13:5?

Bibliography

Barclay, William, *The Daily Study Bible, The Gospel of Matthew Vol. 1*, (The Saint Andrews Press, Edinburgh,1975)

———. *The Daily Study Bible: Ephesians* (Westminster John Knox Press, Louisville, KY, 2004), Commentary on Ephesians

———. *The Ten Commandments*, (Arthur James Ltd, Berkhamstead, 1973)

Bible Hub, *Strongs Concordance* http://biblehub.com/hebrew/2530.htm

Campolo, Anthony, Jr., *The Power Delusion* (Victor Books, Wheaton, Il,1983)

Chesterton, G.K, *The Crimes of England,* (Read Books Ltd, Worcestershire, 2016)

Cosby, Bill; *Fatherhood*, (Doubleday, NY, 1986)

Dobson, J. & Bauer, G; *Children at Risk*, (Word, 1990)

Ezrachints, *Honor Thy Father and Thy Mother,* https://ezrachimts.wordpress.com/2016/08/14/honor-thy-father-and-thy-mother-exodus-20122, *August 14, 2016*

Gibbs, Nancy and Duffy, Michael, *Time: Ruth Graham, Soulmate to Billy, Dies,* http://content.time.com/time/nation/article/0,8599,1633197,00.html

Hengel, Martin. *Property and Riches in the Early Church*, (Fortress, Philadelphia, 1974)

Huie, Jonathan Lockwood, *Inspirational Quotes About Life,* https://www.quotes-inspirational.com/quotes/ beings, Pierre Teilhard de Chardin

Ironside,H.A, *Illustrations of Bible Truth*, (Moody, Il, 1945)

Laurie, Greg, *The Christian Post,* https://www.christianpost.com/news/mean-what-you-say-34602

Lewis, C.S., *AZ Quotes,* http://www.azquotes.com/quote/662866

Lit2Go, *Grimm Brothers—The Old Man and his Grandson* http://etc.usf.edu/lit2go/175/grimms-fairy-tales/3093/the-old-man-and-his-grandson

Lynn, Leslie B, *Now A Word from Our Creator*, (Victor Books, Wheaton, Il, 1976)

McDowell, Josh, *Givers Takers & Other Kinds of Lovers* (Living Books-Tyndale House, Wheaton, Il, 1986)

National Association for Shoplifting Prevention, https://www.shoplifting prevention.org/what-we-do/learning-resource-center/statistics, 2014

New York Times, http://www.nytimes.com/1997/06/21

Quotationsbook.com, *Pope John Paul II,* http://quotationsbook.com/quote/14277

Richard, Cliff, *AZ Quotes,* http://www.azquotes.com/quote/823776

Seller, Jack *"The Pastors Desktop"* (December 30, 2012), http://pastorsdesktop.com/wordpress/morbus-sabbaticus

Solzhenitsyn, Aleksandr, *The Gulag Archipelago* 1918–1956, (Mass Market Paperback, 1974)

Trivette, Ken, *Sermonsearch.* http://www.sermonsearch.com/sermon-outlines/15745/i-love-you-mom-and-dad-6-of-11

———. *Sermonsearch-The Sin That Nobody Confesses as Sin,* http://www.sermonsearch.com/sermon-outlines/15750/the-sin-that-nobody-confesses-as-sin

Urdang and Flexner, *The Random House College Dictionary,* (Random House, NY, 1973)

Vine, W.E, *An Expository Dictionary of New Testament Words,* (Riverside Book and Bible House, Iowa, 1939)

Warner, Rob, *The Ten Commandments and the Decline of the West,* (Kingsway Publications, Eastbourne, 1997)

Wexler, Mark N. , *Successful Resume Fraud: Conjectures on the Origins of Amorality in the Workplace,* Journal of Human Values, Volume: 12 issue: 2, October 2006)

Ziglar Zig, *Sermon Illustrations-Stealing,* http://www.sermonillustrations.com/a-z/s/stealing.htm